British Government Since 1918

First published in 1950, *British Government Since 1918* presents a comprehensive, well-balanced account of the machinery by which public affairs are regulated in Britain. The Institute of Public Administration asked six experts to make a broad survey of the significant happenings in each of the main fields of government. Their names by themselves guarantee the authority and readability of this important book.

Lord Campion deals with the changes in parliamentary procedure; D. N. Chester with the cabinet and its committees; Professor W. J. M. Mackenzie with the central departments; Professor W. A. Robson with the administrative law; Sir Arthur Street with the public corporation and quasi-governmental bodies; and J. H. Warren with local government. This is a must read for students of political science and public administration.

British Government Since 1918

With an Introduction by The Rt. Hon. Sir John
Anderson

Lord Campion, D. N. Chester, W. J. M.
Mackenzie, William A. Robson, Sir Arthur
Street, and J. H. Warren

Routledge
Taylor & Francis Group

First published in 1950
by George Allen & Unwin Ltd.

This edition first published in 2024 by Routledge
4 Park Square, Milton Park, Abingdon, Oxon, OX14 4RN

and by Routledge
605 Third Avenue, New York, NY 10017

Routledge is an imprint of the Taylor & Francis Group, an informa business

© 1950 Lord Campion, D. N. Chester, W. J. M. Mackenzie, William A. Robson, Sir Arthur Street, J. H. Warren

Publisher's Note
The publisher has gone to great lengths to ensure the quality of this reprint but points out that some imperfections in the original copies may be apparent.

Disclaimer
The publisher has made every effort to trace copyright holders and welcomes correspondence from those they have been unable to contact.

A Library of Congress record exists under LCCN: 51000111

ISBN: 978-1-032-88927-6 (hbk)
ISBN: 978-1-003-54041-0 (ebk)
ISBN: 978-1-032-88929-0 (pbk)

Book DOI 10.4324/9781003540410

BRITISH GOVERNMENT
SINCE 1918

LORD CAMPION
D. N. CHESTER
W. J. M. MACKENZIE
WILLIAM A. ROBSON
SIR ARTHUR STREET
J. H. WARREN

*

WITH AN INTRODUCTION BY
THE RT. HON.
SIR JOHN ANDERSON

LONDON
GEORGE ALLEN AND UNWIN LTD
RUSKIN HOUSE · MUSEUM STREET

PRINTED IN GREAT BRITAIN

FIRST PUBLISHED IN 1950
SECOND IMPRESSION 1951
THIRD IMPRESSION 1957

This volume was prepared at the instigation of
THE INSTITUTE OF PUBLIC ADMINISTRATION
76A NEW CAVENDISH STREET
LONDON, W.1

BRITISH GOVERNMENT SINCE 1918

INTRODUCTION BY

THE RT. HON SIR JOHN ANDERSON

The provision of a comprehensive, well balanced and up to date account of the machinery by which public affairs are regulated in this country is of supreme importance to every student of political science, and of interest to every citizen eager to discharge adequately the responsibilities falling upon him under our democratic system.

It is appropriate that such a task should be undertaken under the auspices of the Institute of Public Administration. The ramifications are so wide that the task was bound to be difficult. Though it may appear to some readers that perfect balance has not been achieved, it cannot be doubted that in the result every aspect of the subject has been fully treated, so that no student or general reader need look elsewhere for any information he may require. If I were writing a review, instead of an introduction, I should have much to say that would be out of place here.

The extension of public responsibilities during the past 50 years and the rapid intensification of the process during the last decade makes the book timely, and, indeed, overdue.

It is not surprising to find that enlargement of the scope of public business has led to readjustments in relationship between Parliament and the Executive, and to progressive modifications of Parliamentary procedure designed to facilitate the more expeditious discharge of the tasks thrown upon the legislature. Parliament would have been unequal to those tasks without an extensive delegation of legislative power subject to adequate parliamentary control.

During the same period the central machinery of executive government has been elaborated and systematised. Though the Cabinet still has no legal status it has become an essential organ of Government for ensuring coherence and continuity of policy. Its size and the procedure under which it functions remain entirely flexible.

The complex of authorities constituting the Central Government exhibits a continuous process of redistribution of functions dictated not less by considerations of practical convenience than in deference to *a priori* reasoning. The personnel which at the end of the 19th century was little more than an assemblage of office staffs has been integrated into an organised service.

In a parliamentary democracy public business must, of course, be conducted in accordance with the law as interpreted by properly constituted tribunals. Here a discussion of the increasing resort to delegated legislative and judicial functions is entirely appropriate. How far a study of this subject is facilitated by assigning all law relating to public administration to a separate category of " administrative law "—having nothing to do, needless to say, with the Continental system of " *droit administratif* "—must be a matter of opinion. Criticism would be easy but not in keeping with the character of this note.

Of special interest at the present time is a discussion of the enormous development of the not entirely new device of public Corporations or administrative boards here dealt with under the title of " quasi-government bodies ". A treatment, so comprehensive and authoritative, of what is probably the most striking development in administrative technique of our generation, has never I think been made available before. This alone would justify the present volume if nothing else did.

Finally there is the sphere of local government. It is well to be reminded of the part which local elected authorities have played traditionally in the affairs of this country, and of the changes by way of extension or curtailment of their public responsibilities which modern developments have brought about. It remains as true to-day as it ever was that local self-government is the cradle of democracy, and those who undertake the task of creating machinery appropriate to the discharge of new public responsibilities will neglect this aspect at their peril. They have the less excuse in that the local government service is now an established entity in almost as full a sense as the Civil Service of the Crown.

I commend this symposium to teacher and student alike.

CONTENTS

CHAPTER I

DEVELOPMENTS IN THE PARLIAMENTARY SYSTEM SINCE 1918

by LORD CAMPION, G.C.B.

IN tracing the developments in the parliamentary system since 1918 overmuch attention need not be paid to the war years, 1939 to 1945. These abnormal years certainly provided a test of the adaptability of Parliament. For organized Opposition—the distinctive mark of the system in its normal working—ceased to exist. Both sides of the House supported the Governments in which they were equally represented. Bills which would normally have required many weeks of discussion passed in as many hours. Precedents were created which in other times would be considered unfair to the minority, and are best forgotten. But some war results remain—the habituation of the House to the atmosphere of crisis, and a greater readiness to defer to a masterful Government. The latter is perhaps only the acceleration of a gradual long-term process.

The period under review is thus mainly the inter-war period. But the choice of this period presents an initial difficulty because it is in many respects abnormal and out of the line of previous parliamentary development. For one thing, it was largely a period of coalition government. "England hates a coalition," it is said, and this form of government undoubtedly distorts the working of the House of Commons, because it enfeebles the Opposition and confuses both government and opposition by the formation of dissident groups among the supporters of the Ministry. It also tends to reduce the volume of legislation by restricting it to what can be agreed upon by the parties forming the coalition. In the inter-war period of nearly twenty-one years nearly four years were occupied by Mr. Lloyd George's Coalition Ministry, surviving from the previous war, and eight years by the MacDonald-Baldwin-Chamberlain National Government which carried on into the succeeding war. There were also two periods of minority government—

again a distortion of the parliamentary system—the Labour Administrations of 1924 and 1929-31, which between them occupied three full years. Thus, in the whole period, less than six years were occupied by governments of the normal type (to which the machinery of the House of Commons is primarily adapted)—namely the single-party administration with a working majority. These were the Bonar Law and Baldwin Governments from October 1922 to January 1924 and the second Baldwin Government from November 1924 to June 1929. And even during these administrations the conditions were not quite normal, since the functions of opposition were enfeebled by being divided between Labour and the Liberals, the Liberals themselves being split into two groups.

It is clear that any conclusions drawn from the inter-war period would be very misleading unless they were checked by some other period, such as the period 1906 to 1914, when in spite of the Irish Nationalist third party the parliamentary system was functioning comparatively normally. In this respect the 1945 Parliament is a reversion to the normal type. There is a single-party administration with an adequate majority. There is also a coherent single-party Opposition, the complicating effects of a third party being reduced to negligible proportions. My general line, therefore, in tracing the recent development of the parliamentary system will be to contrast the inter-war period both with the period from 1906 to 1914 and with the present period from 1945, beginning with a brief sketch of the characteristics of the three periods.

It is difficult now to recall the startling impression which the House of Commons elected in January 1906 made on those who had looked on membership as confined more or less to the "governing classes," and on the House itself as expected to live up to its reputation of being the "best club in London." It seems strange now that the composition of the House should then have had a predominantly aristocratic character, when, as far back as 1867 the town artisan, and in 1884 the agricultural labourer, had secured the vote. The electorate was democratic, nearly 70 per cent. of the adult male population being enfranchised. But representation remained aristocratic until 1906. For this there were several reasons. There were still many families whose long traditions of service in the House of Commons made them very formidable opponents, particularly in agricultural constituencies. Then again, as the pendulum swung regularly from Liberal to Tory and back again, membership offered a very precarious career to the individual, which only the rich could afford, particularly as the parliamentary salary was still in the future. All this was changed in 1906. 377 Liberals and Radicals —many of them poor men—besides 83 Irish Nationalists and 29 of the new independent Labour Party, confronted a Conservative Opposition reduced to 157. Previously, Members had used the dining-rooms and terrace chiefly for entertainment. Most of them had houses in the West End. To suit their luncheon and dinner engagements, the House had then begun its sitting at 3.30, adjourned for an interval between 7.30 and 9.0 and wound up business at midnight. These arrangements did not suit the new type of Member at all. He lived perhaps in a distant suburb. When he came down to the House, he intended to remain for the rest of the day, and he wanted to take his ordinary meals there. Thus the Kitchen Committee took to providing cheap meals at a shilling a head; the hour of meeting was advanced to 2.45; and the normal hour of rising to 11 o'clock so that there was time to catch the last train home. Fashionable dinner parties were relegated to a room on the terrace. The seriousness of parliamentary life was emphasized when in 1906 the traditional adjournment over Derby day was discontinued. In 1911, the fact that a large number of Members gave their whole time to the House was recognized in the institution of the parliamentary salary at £400 a year.

These arrangements have persisted to the present time, with little change except during the war. The salary went up to £600 in 1937 and in the 1945-50 Parliament to £1,000. In 1945 the hours of sitting and rising, which had been earlier during the war, became 2.30 and 10.30, respectively; and the hardworking type of Member who is prepared to give most or even all his time to his parliamentary duties, forms a very large percentage of the House in the 1945-50 Parliament. But during

13

the inter-war period there was some reversion to pre-1906 conditions. Conservatives were in a large majority in the Parliaments of 1919 to 1922, 1924 to 1929, and from 1931 till the war. Many of them were active men of business who could not leave their offices or their work in the courts until late in the afternoon. They had to be excused from standing committees which sit in the morning; there was a tendency for all but full-dress debates to be thinly attended; the counting out of the House was not infrequent. The Labour Party, which for the greater part of the time formed the official Opposition, had one serious disqualification for this rôle—they disliked being kept up late. For, if they missed the last trains they had no means of getting home. Keeping the House up late is one of the traditional methods by which the Opposition shows its resentment against unduly heavy pressure by Ministers, and hints that the progress of business should be slowed down. When they were in opposition in 1924 and 1929-31 the Conservatives took a mischievous pleasure in making Government supporters miss the last train; and the latter retaliated by keeping the sitting going until the morning trains were running. Generally speaking, during the inter-war period opposition was ineffective compared with pre-1914 standards, and the Government got through a growing mass of business without much evidence of strain on the machine. In the 1945-50 Parliament an unprecedented spate of business has gone through with unexampled speed. The Opposition does not seem to have settled down systematically to the work of opposing, which involves heavy and thankless toil; and the present temper of party controversy has not reached a level which favours the revival of deliberate obstruction.

The most remarkable change during the last forty years is the fall in the temperature of the party conflict. Between 1906 and 1914 party animosity in the House of Commons reached a degree of virulence which is almost inconceivable to the present generation—in this country, I hasten to add. The burning questions of the hour, the Lloyd George Budget, the quarrel over the "Lords' veto," Home Rule, Votes for Women, aroused the most intense bitterness and fanaticism. In the

House violent scenes of disorder occurred, necessitating the suspension of the sitting. On one occasion an Opposition Front-Bencher, Mr. Ronald McNeill, afterwards Lord Cushendun, assaulted Mr. Churchill across the Table with a well-aimed blow with the "Manual of Public Procedure." At the Derby a suffragette killed herself by dashing on to the course and seizing the reins of the leading horse. As Mr. J. A. Spender puts it "Foreigners, looking on, asked in amazement what had happened to the British people. Where was their ancient sobriety, orderliness and good humour?" Parliamentary government seemed in process of being paralysed by rancour and faction; and in 1914 the country was on the brink of civil war over the question of Ulster.

Then war came from outside, and its very real dangers dissipated the nightmare of internal disruption for good and all. The actors in those disorderly years showed that they had learnt their lesson. During the war, the experience of working together in coalition restored friendly relations between the members of the opposing parties; and this atmosphere survived the war and the problems of its aftermath and has never been seriously interrupted. When it appeared that a group of Scottish Labour Members, elected together in 1922, and nicknamed the "Glasgow Gang" proposed to introduce "real ginger" into the proceedings of the House, there were some awkward and even painful scenes. But that power of disarmament and assimilation, for which the House is famous (assisted by the remarkable patience of Mr. Speaker Whitley) began to work, and in the course of a session or two they had all settled down as good House of Commons men. Several of them, especially James Maxton, became the best-liked men in the House. Quite apart from this special case, it seems to be a fact of British parliamentary experience that the democratisation of the House tends to increase the good temper of Members. At any rate, the standard of orderliness has improved steadily, and the present House has probably shown as high a standard as any.

I propose now to examine the working of the procedure of the House during these periods to see whether it reflects any significant development in what is the basis of the parliamentary system, the relationship between the Government and the House of Commons. In this field, if anywhere—and especially in the arrangements for the distribution of the time of the session— it may be possible to indicate what would otherwise require many chapters of historical analysis. Partisan intolerance of opposition tends to show itself first in moves to tinker with the rules of procedure so as to reduce the opportunities for hostile criticism.

It is generally put forward as a criticism of our system that the Government is unduly predominant over Parliament, and that this predominance has been increasing steadily with each successive extension of the franchise—at least since the second Reform Act of 1867. The argument runs something like this. The huge constituencies which a wide franchise creates need elaborate and extensive machinery to spread the party gospel and bring supporters, and waverers, to the poll. The personality of the ordinary candidate counts for little at a general election, because the party managers find it profitable to focus attention on a few well-known leaders, and the electors have readily learnt to simplify the issues of the contest into a competition between rival Prime Ministers. This depresses the standing of the individual Member. And, in the House itself, parallel machinery, playing upon the Member's party loyalty, turns him into a unit in a highly disciplined force whose main duty is to give unswerving support to the policy of its leaders. Since Ministers are the leaders of the majority party, the success of this doctrine has given them control of the powers properly belonging to Parliament as well as the executive powers which they possess as Ministers of the Crown. The conclusion is that unless there is some relaxation in the stringency of party discipline, on which ministerial power is based, the Government will continue to dominate, and may arrive at dictating to, Parliament. This is not quite how the parliamentary system was intended to work. The House of Commons acquired political power as an organ of control *over* the executive. The question we should ask ourselves is, Is this diagnosis correct hitherto, and, if so, is the position likely to get better or worse?

16

Now it is true that, judging by certain obvious tests, it does look as though the Government tended more and more to act as though they were the sole source of parliamentary action and masters of the House of Commons, responsible only to the electors. Until well after the Reform Act of 1832, Ministers confined themselves almost entirely to the field of administration, and left the initiation of legislation to unofficial Members. Now they have acquired almost a monopoly in both Houses of this traditional function of Parliament. Up to 1868, it was the accepted constitutional doctrine that a Ministry, defeated at the polls, should come back to face the House and take their dismissal at its hands. Now, unless there is some real doubt about the result of an election (as in 1924), the defeated Prime Minister resigns at once and lets his opponents form a government and open Parliament. It seems as if the Government looked over the heads of Members to the electors, and regarded the electorate, and not the House, as their direct masters. Again, until well past the middle of last century, Ministers often left questions of policy to the free vote of the House, whereas now the Whips are "put on" whenever Government policy is concerned, so as to show their supporters that they are expected to follow obediently. And this form of coercion is very effective. Up to about 1865, a majority of the House often ventured to differ from the Government, and the Government would then reshape its policy. Even Palmerston, at the height of his authority from 1859 to 1865, accepted defeat on an average twelve times a session with perfect complacency. Gradually, after 1868, Ministers took to treating almost every question as a question of confidence, and threatened to dissolve or resign if they were defeated in the division lobby. These tactics were entirely successful. By the end of the century a Government defeat had become almost inconceivable. In 1894, Lord Rosebery found it possible to use a snap defeat on a minor issue as a respectable excuse for a resignation which had become desirable on other grounds. The result of this policy, it is concluded, is to reduce the House in matters of Government policy to a registration chamber; debate is unreal because it never changes a vote; whatever the arguments, the result of the division is known

B

beforehand. At most, debate may affect public opinion outside and possibly weaken the Government against the next general election.

If that were the whole truth, the outlook for the parliamentary system would indeed be gloomy. But it is possible that the argument proves too much. If a modern Government is omnipotent in the House of Commons, and if it owes its position to the blind party loyalty of its followers, why does it not take the step which leaders, animated solely by party spirit, have found to be logical in other countries—get rid of its opponents altogether and make its own party the sole party in the state? There is no legal impediment to this, nothing to prevent Parliament by a majority vote putting an end to legal opposition and introducing the single-party system.

The fact that this suggestion sounds fantastic to us proves, I think, that some factor has been left out of account. We do not regard the Government, any Government, as actuated purely by party spirit. We tacitly assume the existence of a counterbalancing factor—call it the "parliamentary spirit." "Parliamentary spirit" is by no means incompatible with "party spirit"—in our system it includes it. For centuries party has been the dynamic, and also the organizing, agency in Parliament, and without party Parliament would fall into impotence and anarchy. But the parliamentary spirit does put a limit to the indulgence of party spirit. In a parliamentary system no party can be completely self-centred. It instinctively avoids doing anything which would destroy the parliamentary system or seriously impede its working. It must at least tolerate the existence of other parties, let the electors vote for them if they wish, and leave them free to express their views in the country and in Parliament.

This is the minimum restraint on party spirit which is indispensable to the existence of the parliamentary system. In England we have gone much further. Whether by historical good luck, in our Whig-Tory dichotomy, or, more likely, through something deeply seated in national character (which shows itself in our legal procedure and even in our attitude to games) we mean by the "party system" *two* organized parties

18

opposing each other. Our system would no longer make sense if one of the opposing parties ceased to exist. It functions badly if one of the parties is permanently weakened, until a new party takes on the vacant rôle. Where more than two organized parties enter the lists one is sooner or later eliminated.

This accounts for the capital importance of the Opposition in the British parliamentary system (and in those Parliaments which have retained its spirit and not merely reproduced its forms)—"His Majesty's Opposition," as it was happily christened more than a hundred years ago, it is said by John Cam Hobhouse. What we mean by the "Opposition" is the party for the time being in the minority, organized as a unit and officially recognized, which has had experience of office and is prepared to form a Government when the existing Ministry has lost the confidence of the country. It must have a positive policy of its own and not merely oppose destructively. Further—this is the crucial difference from the French system—the line of party cleavage must cut the field of politics somewhere near the centre. We are not used to anything, except at the most a handful of extremists, either to the right of the Tories or to the left of Labour. Where, as in France, the Ministry is almost inevitably drawn from the parties of the centre, no co-operation can be established between the mutually hostile opposition parties of the Right and the Left, except for purposes of destruction. Our system, alone, can produce a responsible Opposition, one with a consistent policy known to the country in broad outline, one which is not anxious to win at the expense of ruining the game.

Incidentally, it must be admitted that although the two-party antithesis is the normal form of the British parliamentary system and one to which by hook or by crook it ultimately returns, it is a rule which has not been realized in practice without many exceptions. During four periods of substantial length third parties have introduced an element of confusion into British party politics,—the Peelites in the middle of the nineteenth century, the Liberal Unionists for twenty years after 1885, the Irish Nationalists from 1874 to 1918, and finally the see-saw of Liberal and Labour from 1918 until the Liberals ceased to count as a potential Government party during the inter-war period. The Peelites and Liberal Unionists were parties of leaders which soon ceased to have independent voting support. The Irish Nationalists were more dangerous, for they felt no responsibility to the parliamentary system, and indeed wished only to destroy it, although they had been to a large extent "acclimatized"—to their own undoing—before their final elimination in the Irish Free State. The Liberal débâcle, which prolonged itself throughout the inter-war period, began as a struggle with Labour for the second place—the right to constitute the official Opposition. Nothing shows more clearly than the fate of this great party that opposition alone is not sufficient, and that acceptance by the electorate as a potential alternative Government is necessary to the survival of a party. Nor does anything show more clearly how effectively our system in the long run eliminates deviations from the normal, however respectable, and how intolerant it is of more than two occupants of its procrustean double-bed.

The practice of the House of Commons emphasizes the importance of the official Opposition in every possible way. This is right because under modern conditions it has fallen to the Opposition to discharge what was regarded before the institution of Cabinet Government as the primary function of the House as a whole—the control by criticism of the executive. Its leader is paid a salary out of the Consolidated Fund, and is thus beyond the reach of a majority vote without formal legislation. It is organized like the government party, with a "shadow" Cabinet and Whips of its own. It has its own rights over the time of the House. A word is necessary to show how time is provided for the Opposition. Apart from being consulted as to the length of time required for the discussion of the various stages of Government measures, the Opposition has by a convention of about fifty years standing the right to choose the subjects to be debated on the days allotted to the consideration of the Estimates and the bills by which they are finally authorized. According to modern practice this means that the Opposition has the right to initiate discussion of any branch of administration on about 32 days in each session. In addition the Government is morally bound to grant a day for the discussion of any vote of censure which the Opposition wish to move. The Opposition leaders also have the right to choose the subjects to be debated on certain items of business of a very general kind (in which the procedure of the House abounds) such as the Address in reply to the King's Speech, motions for the adjournment of the House, and even certain stages of the Budget. An attempt will be made at the end of this Paper to estimate the average amount of time each session which the Opposition controls in this way. It is very substantial. On the whole it is fair to say that the initiative in criticism which is enjoyed by the Opposition is by far the most important modern element in freedom of debate, and that its preservation is something which the country should value as a guarantee against any form of totalitarianism—as a real check on the further growth of ministerial autocracy in Parliament. It would be the clearest proof of the triumph of party spirit over parliamentary spirit if any government set out to whittle away the rights of the Opposition.

The hardening-up of the party system since the middle of the nineteenth century—a process which has turned all but a few "Independents" into loyal members of the party in office or the party in opposition—could not fail to have a disastrous effect on the status and functions of the individual "private" Member (strictly a Member who does not hold office, but often synonymous with "back-bencher"—a Member who is neither a Minister nor one of the leading Members of the Opposition). Up to a hundred years ago most legislation was introduced by private Members. Even bills of first class importance—one thinks of Wilberforce and the abolition of the slave trade, or Ashley and the reform of factory conditions. The private Member enjoyed all the time of the House which was not explicitly allotted to the Government. At the beginning of the nineteenth century the House allowed the Government two days a week for their business. By the middle of the century this had grown to three days. But private Members long enjoyed their two days a week, though Ministers acquired the habit of appropriating one or even both days towards the end of the session on the ground of urgent business. In 1906 the Campbell-Bannerman Government introduced the change which gave all the time of the House to the Government, except two evenings a week and the short Friday sitting—and this concession was limited to what usually amounted to the first two months of the session. During the war of 1914-1918 the Government appropriated private Members' time on the plea of urgency. It was restored for the greater part of the inter-war period, but was again appropriated during the last war, and the present Government shows no disposition to restore it.*

It seems that there is no urgent conviction even among private Members of the value of Private Members' time. No one can truthfully say that private Members made the best use of their opportunities. The luck of the ballot often resulted in the presentation of what were called "wild cat schemes" or "hardy annuals." Sometimes on the other hand these bills emanated from Government departments via the Whips' Office. Unless they were non-contentious, insufficient time was provided for the later stages of these bills, and very few in fact passed session by session. If they did, it was generally due to the favour of Ministers—as in the case of Mr. Herbert's Matrimonial Causes Bill and Sir Ralph Glyn's Race-course Betting Bill. With regard to Private Members' Motions the position was somewhat better, though they were often inspired by one of the front benches, and if not, were seldom of sufficient interest to attract a full House. Counting out was frequent on Private Members' days. Nevertheless it would be a loss to the procedure of the House if Private Members' time were not restored, at least in part. It provides the most important of the few parliamentary opportunities which, in particular, the back-bench supporter of the Government enjoys of raising matters outside the party programme. It has in the past proved useful for ventilating subjects, such as women's rights, which cut across party lines; and it could be used in the future to afford an outlet for independent views which do not find favour with either front bench, and which under present conditions can only be forwarded by

* In 1948/49 ten Fridays were allotted for Private Members' Bills.

extra-parliamentary pressure. It is intelligible, however, in a party-ridden House that the Government do not feel themselves under the same obligation to preserve Private Members' rights as those of the Opposition, and find they can encroach on the former, as they could not on the latter, without being charged with attempting to "muzzle" the House.

After these preliminary observations of a somewhat elementary character, let us return to the question whether, and if so to what extent, the ascendancy of the Government over Parliament has continued to grow since 1918, as compared with the period from 1906 to 1914. Changes in procedure directed to expediting Government business will be noted, and the figures of the distribution of time will be examined, to see if they show any significant reduction in the opportunities traditionally allowed to the Opposition and to the House generally for the expression of minority views.

1906 to 1914. The Campbell-Bannerman Government faced the new Parliament with the second largest majority since 1833. The Liberal Party was considerably more than half the House, and in addition it could count on the general support of about 80 Nationalists and 29 of the new Independent Labour group. The Conservative Opposition of about 150 was disorganized by the loss of many of its leaders, including the ex-Prime Minister Arthur Balfour. This unwieldy majority was by no means a blessing, for it encouraged the formation of groups within the party which pressed their own policies undeterred by the salutary fear of an Opposition victory. To give one example, the Government were forced by their followers to withdraw their Trades Disputes Bill in favour of the more extreme measure put forward by the trade unions, to which a majority of their supporters had pledged themselves during the preceding election.

In their reform of procedure the Government, besides lengthening the working hours of the House, introduced a number of devices for accelerating the passage of their legislation. They established four "standing" committees for considering the details of bills, thus saving the time of the whole House at the expense of excluding all but a comparatively small proportion of Members from what to the average Member is the most important stage of a bill. They made an intensified use of the drastic closure rule; empowered the Chair on occasion to disallow amendments however unobjectionable on grounds of order; and brought into systematic use the device, which had only occasionally been resorted to before, of applying time-tables to the stages of bills, with the result that important clauses could be voted without discussion—the so-called "Guillotine" procedure. Further, by restricting the "veto" of the House of Lords, which had been used (without much discretion) by the Conservative Party, and thus removing all restraint on the legislative power of a majority of the House of Commons, the Asquith Ministry in effect greatly enhanced the ascendancy of the Government in control of such a majority over the House of Commons itself. By their procedural changes, it cannot be denied, the Liberal Government of this period substantially reduced the rights of the House to criticize Government measures. They did not, however, interfere with the opportunities accorded by practice to the Opposition of choosing subjects on which to criticize Government administration.

1918 to 1939. The inter-war period—a period of intermittent crises, marked throughout by industrial depression and labour unrest and over-shadowed towards the end by German re-armament and aggression—was hardly favourable to the normal working of the parliamentary system. With regard especially to the relations between Government and the House of Commons the deviations from the normal were most marked. The Lloyd-George Coalition Government of 1918 had little to fear from the attacks of an Opposition, weak and divided between Labour and Asquith Liberals. But it had to face the growing discontent of the great Conservative mass of its supporters which at last broke away and destroyed it in 1922. The short-lived Conservative Parliament of 1923 was of the normal type, but the Labour Government of 1924 was abnormal in two respects. Its leaders had no experience of office as a single-party Administration; and it was a minority Government, prepared, like the mid-nineteenth century Governments, to accept defeat on all but vital issues—it was in fact defeated some dozen times before Ramsay MacDonald secured the dissolution of Parliament. The Parliament of 1925-1929 was closer to the normal type—it had a single-party Government with a substantial majority—but the Opposition was divided and ineffective. It was followed by the Parliament of 1929-1931, led by the second minority Labour Government, which broke down under the economic crisis of 1931 with the secession of its principal leaders. The National Government of 1931-1935 enjoyed almost unlimited parliamentary power, even after it shed its small Liberal contingent. For the continuing economic stringency kept the ranks of its supporters united, (though there were complaints against the strictness of party discipline) and the Labour Opposition was weak in numbers and disheartened by a resounding failure in office and by the loss of its leaders. It was this Parliament which accepted what would have been considered an incredible inroad on the traditional rights of the House of Commons—its exclusive right to grant taxes—by delegating powers to impose import duties by administrative order. The Parliament of 1935 saw a renewal of vigorous opposition against the National Government, now almost entirely Conservative, at the hands of a Labour Opposition considerably increased in numbers, and also at the hands of its own supporters, who, sometimes in conjunction with the Opposition (as in the case of the Hoare-Laval Treaty) and sometimes separately, secured many important concessions from the Government. After 1939, in this Parliament far more than in the Parliament of 1914-1918, the exigencies of war had the effect of associating the Opposition parties with office, of stilling the voice of criticism, and of reconciling the House of Commons to the grant of almost dictatorial powers to the Government.

It might be thought that the variations in the relative strength and weakness of Government and Opposition during the inter-war period were so extreme that no definite conclusion could be drawn as to whether the ascendancy of the Government over the House of Commons was on the whole advancing beyond the stage reached in 1914 or receding. On the whole, it seems, this was a period of marking time. One must take account of the fact that the trend towards the predominance of the executive was well established and reflected in arrangements for the conduct of business with which the Chair and Members generally were familiar—a fact which operated so as to "iron out" extreme variations and bring them back towards the normal. The control and support of the whole machinery of administration is a powerful re-inforcement for the weakest Government; and a sense of responsibility in the Opposition somewhat relaxes the narrow bounds within which a government ostensibly restricted to non-controversial legislation can operate. On the other hand the powerful traditions of debate, embodied in the standing orders and supported by accepted conventions, make it a serious matter—an open muzzling of Parliament—for the most autocratic Government to take the positive steps required to restrict the opportunities allowed, particularly to the official Opposition, for raising subjects of censure and criticism. The inexperienced minority Government of 1924 got through a respectable amount of legislation; and the all-powerful National Government of 1931 did nothing to cut down "Opposition Time" (see below), although private Members were deprived of their opportunities for a session or two. During the period from 1931 the established methods of restricting debate—the closure and the guillotine—were rarely resorted to, and a new precedent was introduced in the form of a "voluntary" time-table which was applied with the consent of all parties to the most elaborate and potentially controversial measure of this period, the Government of India Bill.

1939 to 1945. Except for the fact that they familiarized Ministers and Members with autocratic methods and thus had an influence on the post-war period, the war years can be left out of account in a study of the relations between Parliament and executive under normal conditions. Extraordinary powers of control over the life of the nation, conferred almost without debate, the suppression in the interest of public security of information essential to criticism, together with the reluctance of Members generally to embarrass the Government deprived the House of much of its ordinary material for debate, especially after the formation of Mr. Churchill's Coalition Government. This was reflected in a shorter sitting day and a reduction in the number of sittings. Although Private Members' time was taken, the Government were careful to preserve the forms and conventions which guaranteed the rights of the Opposition, and to permit freer debate than was possible in the open House by extending the system of secret sessions introduced in the previous war. On the whole, with exceptions which were easily remediable, the House emerged from the war with its rules intact. The chief change was that Members had grown accustomed to high-handed methods and half-persuaded of the necessity of their retention.

1945–50. The Labour Government came into office as the beneficiaries of the war-mentality of the previous Parliament. They found little of that desire on the part of Members to get rid of all war-time controls which had so hampered the Government of 1919. Instead, it was generally expected that, in the necessary overhaul of procedure that was bound to take place, some new devices would be introduced to speed up the passage of Government business. A Select Committee on Procedure was appointed in October 1945 and reappointed the next session. It issued three Reports but recommended few changes beyond a more systematic use of the days allotted to supply (which provide the Opposition with their chief opportunites for initiating debates of criticism). The Government accepted this suggestion, somewhat cutting down the number of days recommend by the Committee. They also pressed through their own proposals for accelerating business, which had been rejected by the Committee, consisting mainly of the reduction of opportunities of debate on the Budget and in committee on a bill. In addition they increased the number of standing committees, and for the first time applied the "Guillotine" procedure to bills under the consideration of these bodies.

Against the recommendation of the Select Committee they refused to consider "for the present" the restoration to private Members of the time reserved by the standing orders which they had appropriated throughout the war.

We can now proceed to check our impressions with regard to the periods examined in the previous pages by seeing whether any conclusions can be drawn from variations in the amount of time allotted each session to Government business, Opposition business and Private Members' business respectively.

During the period 1906 to 1913, in a session of the average length of 145 days Government business occupied on the average 63 days, Opposition business 44½ days, and Private Members' business 20 days. (We may leave out of account 17½ days used for recurrent business including the annual budget which, owing to the peculiar rules under which it is conducted, cannot be brought under any of our three categories.)

During the whole inter-war period the average length of the session was also 145 days. Government business took 61¼ days, Opposition business 46½ days, Private Members' business 20 days. If the inter-war period is divided at 1931 (the date of the resignation of the second Labour Government) the figures tell a somewhat different story.

1919 to 1931. Average length of session 133 days; Government business 52½ days, Opposition business 46½ days, Private Members' business 19 days.

1932 to 1938. Average length of session 158 days; Government business 70½ days, Opposition business 46¼ days, Private Members' business 22 days.

The variations in the distribution of time during these two periods seem very slight. But if the figures are looked at session by session it will be found that, while Opposition time remains fairly constant at about 40 to 45 days, Private Members' time varies considerably with the inroads made upon it by Government demands. Government time varies most of all. An unusually high figure for Government time during a particular session is obtained either by increasing the length of the session beyond the average as in 1908 (Government time 85 days out of 170), 1912-13 (119 days out of 204), 1929-30 (76 out of 185), 1930-31 (81 out of 185) or by combining this with the expedient of appropriating Private Members' time as in 1931-33 (65 days out of 150), 1934-35 (84 out of 150). Opposition time remained intact during these sessions, as it did also in the unusually short sessions of 1922, 1923 and 1928 when the House sat 113, 111 and 113 days respectively and the time reserved by the Government for their programme fell to $28\frac{1}{2}$, 34 and 29 days respectively—actually less than the number of days allotted to the Opposition.

The first two sessions of the present Parliament show, as might be expected, figures for Government time considerably higher than the average, the time spent on Government bills alone being 86 days in 1945/46, and 78 in 1946/47—30 days and 22 days, respectively, above the average. These increases were obtained (apart from the appropriation of Private Members' time) by increasing the length of the session to 207 days in the first session and 163 in the second—60 days and 15 days above the average, respectively. Opposition time was also increased during these sessions to 54 days in the first session and 46 days in the second—10 days and 2 days, respectively, above the average.

These figures, admittedly, do not show the full extent of the increased demands made by the Government on the time of the House and the increasing pressure put upon Members. Account must be taken of the prolongation of the sitting beyond the normal hour, which has been unusually frequent during these sessions; and also of the intensified use that has been made of standing committees, which have been increased in number and worked at very high pressure. To assess these factors would require additional figures which would unduly complicate this paper. But a rough and ready impression of all the factors combined may be obtained by considering variations in the speed with which legislation is forced through the House. In the period 1906 to 1913 the House got through 5 pages on an average on every day on which it considered bills. In 1919 to 1931 the average had risen to 11 pages, and in 1933 to 1938 to 13 pages. In the session 1945/46 the average rose to 16 pages. This gives some idea of the pressure put upon the present House, and possibly indicates a real degree of restriction of the opportunities afforded for the criticism of Government measures. It may well be that the increase in pressure is even greater than it appears from a comparison with the inter-war period. For the relatively high speed of the legislative process during that period, as compared with the period 1906 to 1913, was no doubt due in part to the decline in efficiency as well as in numerical strength of the Opposition during most of the Parliaments of the inter-war period.

That the government of the day (Conservative or Labour) which is nominally in entire control of the time of the House should find itself bound to restrict itself for its own business to an allotment of time which works out on the average to about 43 per cent. of the whole time of the session (39 per cent. for its own programme of legislation) while surrendering over 30 per cent. to the Opposition for choosing subjects on which to criticise the Government—that no Government has felt prepared to defy the rules and conventions which establish these proportions (though it has full legal power to do so)—these facts seem to afford sufficient proof not only of the fairness of the rules and conventions but also of the persistence of the parliamentary spirit which established them, and which remains the best check on the dominance of a single party.

CHAPTER II

DEVELOPMENT OF
THE CABINET 1914—1949

by D. N. Chester, c.b.e., m.a. (*Admin.*)

President Lawrence Lowell started his chapter on the Cabinet in this manner: "A German professor in a lecture on anatomy is reported to have said to his class, 'Gentlemen, we now come to the spleen. About the functions of the spleen, gentlemen, we know nothing. So much for the spleen.' It is with such feelings that one enters upon the task of writing a chapter upon the cabinet." That was written in 1908. I do not know what developments have taken place in medical knowledge since that date but certainly something more than nothing is known nowadays of the functioning of the Cabinet. During the war of 1914-1918, for example, the War Cabinet issued two reports mainly, it is true, concerned with the course of the war but also saying something about developments in Cabinet machinery. During the war of 1939-45 statements were made from time to time in the House of Commons about the use of Cabinet committees. Moreover, we have had since 1938 Sir Ivor Jennings' standard volume—"Cabinet Government." And from biographies of Ministers, and in various other ways our knowledge of the manner in which the Cabinet works has been enlarged. Indeed I have the impression that there is now much less secrecy in the process than when Lowell wrote, and certainly much less than when Bagehot wrote his classic chapter. Nevertheless it is still the most mysterious part of British Government, the inner temple, the high place in which the major decisions of policy are made. It is not easy, therefore, to survey fully the changes which have occurred in Cabinet machinery during the past 25-30 years.

The most obvious data available are the number of Ministers in the Cabinet at any time and the offices they hold. It is worth while examining these figures for at least two reasons. First, with the growth of Government activity has gone a marked increase in the number of departments. This increase has raised the difficult question of whether all Ministers should be included in the Cabinet; if not, which should be left out; and, if they are left out, how is the Cabinet to perform its major function of co-ordinating Government policy over all the many fields of action. Second, the most appropriate size of the Cabinet has been a subject of considerable controversy, at least since Lloyd George's War Cabinet of 1916-19. The following table shows the fluctuations which have occurred in the size of the Cabinet since the beginning of the present century.

SIZE OF CABINET DURING 1901-1949

Period	Prime Minister	Size of Cabinet Range
1901-2	Salisbury	20
1902-5	Balfour	17-19
1905-8	Campbell-Bannerman	19-20
1908-15	Asquith	19-20
1915-16	Asquith	22-22
1916-19	Lloyd George	5-7
1919-22	Lloyd George	18-22
1922-23	Bonar Law	16
1923	Baldwin	19-20
1924	Ramsay MacDonald	20
1924-29	Baldwin	20-21
1929-31	Ramsay MacDonald	19-21
1931	Ramsay MacDonald	10
1931-35	Ramsay MacDonald	19-20
1935-37	Baldwin	20-22
1937-39	Neville Chamberlain	21-23
1939-40	Neville Chamberlain	8-9
1940-45	Churchill	5-9
1945	Churchill	16
1945-	Attlee	16-20

So far as size is concerned Cabinets in this period can be divided into two main categories—the abnormal Cabinets which existed during 1916-19, 1931 and 1939-45 and the normal Cabinets which existed at all other times. Dealing with the latter first, the normal size between 1901 and the outbreak of war in 1914 was 19 (with short periods at 17, 18 and at 20). Between the end of Lloyd George's War Cabinet and the establishment of Neville Chamberlain's the normal size had increased to 20-22—the latter figure tending to be characteristic of the immediate pre-1939-45 war period. Mr. Attlee's government started with 20 members, was reduced to 18 after a year and has been 17 since May 1948.

These figures give the impression that little or nothing had happened during the period and that the task of Cabinet formation was little different in 1948 from 1901. Mr. Attlee's original choice of 20 members in 1945 was exactly the number chosen by Lord Salisbury in 1901, by Mr. Asquith in 1908, by Mr. Baldwin in 1923 and by Mr. Ramsay MacDonald in 1930. Yet his problem was both different and more difficult, for in 1945 there were several more Ministerial posts to be considered for inclusion.

The following 12 Ministerial posts of possible Cabinet rank existed in 1949[1] but not in 1901

Name of Ministry[2]	Year
Education	1902[3]
Labour (& National Service)	1916
Pensions	1916
Air	1918
Transport	1919
Dominions	1925
Supply	1939[4]
Food	1939[4]
Fuel & Power	1942
Town & Country Planning	1943
National Insurance	1944
Civil Aviation	1944

[1]When Mr. Attlee took office in July 1945, there were four departments in existence which subsequently disappeared, viz: Burma, India, Aircraft Production and Information.

[2]Certain departments have changed the title of their Minister, i.e. Agriculture & Fisheries, Education, and Works. I have also assumed the Minister of Health to be the same post as the President of the Local Government Board.

[3]The first President of the Board of Education was appointed in August 1902. Prior to that the Department had a Vice-President as head under the Lord President of the Council.

[4]A Ministry of Munitions and a Ministry of Food Control were established during the war of 1914-18 but were abolished shortly afterwards.

During the same period, however, two Ministerial posts disappeared: Secretary of State for India and the Chief Secretary for Ireland.

Prior to 1920 there also existed a Lord Chancellor of Ireland and a Lord Lieutenant, but it was unusual for them to be in the Cabinet. They were both, however, in the Conservative Administration of 1901-5.

A first question, therefore, is how is it that the Cabinet has not increased in size to the full extent of the increase in the number of Ministerial posts. Let us first compare Lord Salisbury's 1901 Cabinet and Mr. Attlee's 1945 Cabinet:

Ministers in the 1901 Cabinet but not in 1945 Cabinet (Attlee's)	*Ministers in 1945 (Attlee's) Cabinet but not in 1901 Cabinet*
Lord Lieutenant of Ireland	Minister of Labour & National Service
Lord Chancellor of Ireland	Secretary of State for Air
Postmaster General	Secretary of State for Dominions
Chancellor of the Duchy of Lancaster	Minister of Fuel & Power
First Commissioner of Works	Minister of Education

It will be seen that the five new Ministers in the 1945 Cabinet were created after the turn of the century (assuming that the Department of Education could not be regarded as a Ministerial post before August 1902). They replaced two posts abolished in 1920 and displaced three posts still in existence.

Mr. Attlee's 1945 Cabinet can also be compared with Mr. Asquith's 1914 Cabinet of exactly the same size.

Ministers in 1914 Cabinet but not in 1945 (Attlee's) Cabinet	*Ministers in 1945 (Attlee's) Cabinet but not in 1914 Cabinet*
Chief Secretary for Ireland	Secretary of State for Scotland
Postmaster General	Secretary of State for Dominions
Chancellor of the Duchy of Lancaster	Secretary of State for Air
First Commissioner of Works	Minister of Labour & National Service
Attorney General	Minister of Fuel & Power

Mr. Attlee managed to reduce the 20 members of his original Cabinet to 17 members in two ways: by leaving out the heads of the three service departments and including the Minister of Defence as a separate Minister,[1] and by the abolition of the India Office consequent upon India becoming an independent member of the Commonwealth. Later, when the Minister of Fuel and Power ceased to be in the Cabinet after August 1947, the number fell to 16, but reverted to 17 when the Chancellor of the Duchy of Lancaster became a member in May 1948.

The interesting thing about this post-1939-45 Cabinet is not that it differs substantially in membership from the pre-1914 Cabinets. Some departments have changed their names a little. Ireland no longer has one or two representatives in the Cabinet and two or three new departments have managed to get a firm foothold. But the Marquess of Salisbury and Mr. Asquith would find that the great majority of posts in their Cabinets are still in the present-day Cabinet. The big difference is that whereas in their Cabinets all departments were represented, there were many important departments left out of the 1945 Cabinet, and even more out of the 1949 Cabinet.

The following 9 departments were left out of Mr. Attlee's 1945 Cabinet: Ministers of Food, Works, Civil Aviation, Town and Country Planning, Transport, Supply, National Insurance, Pensions and the Postmaster General, and a further four were excluded by the end of 1948: Secretary of State for Air, Secretary of State for War, First Lord of the Admiralty and the Minister of Fuel and Power. In other words, by the end of 1948 and throughout 1949 there were 13 important departments not directly represented in the Cabinet. To these may be added the office of Attorney-General which had been included in the Cabinet during 1912-16 and 1921-27.

It will be noticed that with the exception of the three Service Ministers (replaced by a Minister of Defence) and the Postmaster General the Ministers left out of the Cabinet are all comparatively new offices. Six of the remaining nine have been created since 1939 and only Works existed before 1914. It may, of course, be that the older Ministries are old because the

[1] Mr. Attlee had been his own Minister of Defence until October 1946.

35

subjects with which they deal have been important enough for a long time to warrant special Government attention. But it rather looks as though entry to the Cabinet tends to be by precedent and that the new departments have to struggle for some time before receiving such recognition. It is difficult, for example, to believe that in 1949 either Fuel and Power or Food were less vital to the nation or to the success of the Government than, say, Education or Colonies. Perhaps, however, this is but an illustration of the problem of where to draw the line. For if all departments were included the 1949 Cabinet would contain 30 ministers, and even those who dislike the idea of a small Cabinet of say 5-8 Ministers seldom wish to press their opposition to the extent of having it composed of 30 members.

The Prime Minister in deciding the size of his Cabinet in normal times must have several points in mind. Factors making for a large size are: the desirability of including as many as possible of the leading members of his Parliamentary Party so that what the Cabinet decides is in line with Party opinion in the House; the better co-ordination which is likely to be achieved both in the formation of general Government policy and in the administration of that policy if all the main departments are represented; and the avoidance of possible jealousies and friction between those Ministers who are in and those who are outside the Cabinet. Factors in favour of a small Cabinet are: greater ease in arranging meetings at times when all can be present; greater possibility of reaching speedy decisions not merely because there are fewer Ministers who may wish to talk but, perhaps more important, because a small group is more easy to weld into a team; and the undesirability of taking busy Ministers too frequently and for too long from their departments in order to sit in a Committee discussing items which may be of importance to them either only indirectly or generally. It would appear that the balance of these factors leads to a cabinet of 18 to 20 in normal times.

The three small Cabinets occurred in 1916-19, 1930 and 1939-45. Mr. Lloyd George managed to get along with a Cabinet of 5 to 7 members, and though Mr. Churchill started with 5 members in May 1940 this did not last long and the more usual size was 8 or 9, which was also Mr. Neville Chamberlain's choice. Mr. Ramsay MacDonald had 10 members in his 1931 Coalition Cabinet. It is very noticeable that almost all these small Cabinets have two characteristics: they occur in times of major national crises and during coalitions of the major parties.[1] The crisis gives a note of urgency and usually requires the whole powers of the Government to be directed towards one clear object. Equally important is the fact that it is government by coalition of the major parties. True this is only likely to happen during a serious national crisis, but the fact that it does happen makes a smaller Cabinet more feasible. For it is clear to all that every person who might get office if his party were in power cannot do so in a coalition, for the offices have to be shared with one or more other parties. In these circumstances it is probably easier and more expedient to include only the three or four dominant politicians on each side, for in any party there are usually three or four leaders who stand head and shoulders above the rest.

Even if, however, such small Cabinets are to be confined to times of serious crisis it is now clear that all departments are not in the foreseeable future likely to be represented in the Cabinet. There are likely to be ten or more excluded. This would hardly have been considered proper or good Government in the beginning of the century. What has happened to make it both possible and generally accepted? Probably the answer is to be found in two developments: (1) the institution of a system of Cabinet minutes, the circulation of agenda and papers and the establishment of a Cabinet Secretariat specially for this work; and (2) the establishment of a pattern of Cabinet Committees.

CABINET SECRETARIAT

The story of the institution of Cabinet minutes and agenda and of the Secretariat has been told many times.[2] Before

[1] I assume for this purpose that Mr. Neville Chamberlain's War Cabinet, September 1939 to May 1940, was Conservative and not a Coalition. At least it was not a Coalition of major parties.
[2] See Lord Hankey—*Diplomacy by Conference*, and Sir Ivor Jennings—*Cabinet Government*.

December 1916 the situation in the well-known words of Lord Curzon was as follows :

"There was no agenda, there was no order of business. Any Minister requiring to bring up a matter either of departmental or of public importance had to seek the permission of the Prime Minister to do so. No one else, broadly speaking, was warned in advance. It was difficult for any Minister to secure an interstice in the discussion in which he could place his own case. No record whatever was kept of our proceedings, except the private and personal letter written by the Prime Minister to the Sovereign, the contents of which, of course, are never seen by anybody else. The Cabinet often had the very haziest notion as to what its decisions were; and I appeal not only to my experience, but to the experience of every Cabinet Minister who sits in this House, and to the records contained in the memoirs of half a dozen Prime Ministers in the past, that cases frequently arose when the matter was left so much in doubt that a Minister went away and acted upon what he thought was a decision which subsequently turned out to be no decision at all, or was repudiated by his colleagues. No one will deny that a system, however embedded in the traditions of the past and consecrated by constitutional custom, which was destined immediately it came into contact with the hard realities of war, to crumble into dust at once . . . and to make a long story short, I do not think anyone will deny that the old Cabinet system had irretrievably broken down, both as a war machine, and as a peace machine."[1]

In quoting Lord Curzon, Lord Hankey, the first Secretary of the Cabinet, added: "To the evidence of experienced statesmen it must be added that civil servants often found difficulty in ascertaining from Ministers that decisions had been taken which affected their departments, either because the Minister (especially if new to office) did not always know that his department was concerned or what was the decision."[2]

Up to the time when Mr. Lloyd George succeeded Mr. Asquith as Prime Minister the general management of the war had been in the hands of a combination of a normal-sized

[1]*House of Lords Debates*, Vol. xxx, Col. 265.
[2]Hankey, *Diplomacy by Conference*, p. 54.

Cabinet and an adaptation of the Committee of Imperial Defence. The latter, whether it was called the War Council, Dardanelles Committee, or War Committee, continued the procedure established by the Committee of Imperial Defence: for example, it had a Secretary who attended the meetings and took minutes which were circulated to members. Mr. Lloyd George fused the work of the Cabinet and War Committee into a War Cabinet of five members. This body took over not only the business of the War Committee but also the secretariat and the procedure developed by the Committee of Imperial Defence "including agenda papers, the distribution (in advance of the meetings) of relevant memoranda and other material, the rapid communication of decisions to those who had to act upon them or were concerned in the second degree. . . ."[1]

The Haldane Committee on the Machinery of Government reporting in 1918 considered the wartime experience and said: ". . . we think there is one feature in the procedure of the War Cabinet which may well assume a permanent form, namely, the appointment of a Secretary to the Cabinet charged with the duty of collecting and putting into shape its agenda, of providing the information and the material necessary for its deliberations, and of drawing up records of the results for communication to the departments concerned."[2]

Not everybody agreed with this view, Mr. Asquith in particular being very sceptical of the need to continue the Cabinet secretariat. But the system had proved itself and Ministers who had experience of both systems were definitely in favour of the secretariat. And so even though the Committee of Imperial Defence was re-established in November 1919 the Cabinet did not revert to the pre-1916 system, for the Secretary of that Committee continued also as Secretary to the Cabinet. This decision to have the two offices in the same hands was partly a tribute to Sir Maurice Hankey and partly a recognition that in large measure the two jobs were but aspects of the same main function. When Sir Maurice Hankey retired in July 1938 his successor Sir Edward Bridges was appointed Secretary of the

[1] Hankey, p. 57.
[2] Cd.9230, p. 6.

Cabinet and General H. L. Ismay was appointed Secretary of the Committee of Imperial Defence. The Committee's secretariat was, however, part of the staff of the Cabinet Offices of which Sir Edward Bridges was made head.

In September 1939 the Committee of Imperial Defence was merged in the War Cabinet and its secretariat became part of the War Cabinet secretariat. The War Cabinet secretariat therefore had a military and a civil side, the former staffed by service officers and the latter by the administrative class, both working under the Secretary of the War Cabinet. During the War it was found convenient to house certain specialized functions of a central character in the offices of the War Cabinet—the Economic Section, the Central Statistical Office and certain Supply secretariats.

When in 1945 the Cabinet reverted to its pre-war size, the Committee of Imperial Defence was not reconstituted. The Cabinet secretariat lost some of its functions when the Ministry of Defence was created at the end of 1946, but otherwise continued as before.

How is the institution of Cabinet Minutes and a Secretariat related to the possible size of the Cabinet? Prior to 1916 any Minister who was not a member of the Cabinet found it very difficult to know what had been decided. (This was also true of any Cabinet Minister who for one reason or another could not attend a particular meeting.) Therefore non-attendance at Cabinet meetings did not merely mean that one had not had a chance to state one's views, it might also mean ignorance of what had been decided. Presumably the Prime Minister took it upon himself or arranged with another Minister to inform any Minister not present at the meeting of what had been decided in so far as it had a direct bearing on his department. But it is clear that this would have been an impossible burden on the Prime Minister if he had to do this for a number of Ministers.

Moreover, whilst on many occasions it would be quite clear that this or that matter was the direct concern of a particular Minister, on many other occasions the connection might not be so obvious. As the field of Government activity extends there are few matters which do not affect, directly or indirectly, several

40

departments: in some cases only the Minister and his advisers in the department will be able to say whether the matters concern them or not. The system of agenda, papers circulated in advance, and minutes makes it possible for the Minister and department excluded from the Cabinet to keep in touch with what is happening without imposing any burden on the Prime Minister. For agenda, papers and minutes can be circulated to all Ministers whether or not they are in the Cabinet. If a non-Cabinet Minister finds a paper is to be discussed which affects his department he can ask to be allowed to attend and the Prime Minister will usually give his permission. Again by reading the minutes he can keep in touch with matters discussed and decisions reached at Cabinet meetings even though he has not been present.

Minutes and agenda become even more important if the Cabinet is to operate through a system of committees. For though it might be possible for Ministers to keep in touch with the happenings in the Cabinet without such aids it would be virtually impossible for them to keep in touch with several Cabinet committees as well. And nowadays the task is even more difficult because of the greater frequency of meetings and the wider range of topics. It is noticeable that the keeping of minutes, etc., started with the Committee of Imperial Defence which had numerous sub-committees.

Altogether then, exclusion from the Cabinet means much less now than it did in say 1914, at least so far as being in the know is concerned. On matters which are clearly and directly of concern to his department the Minister excluded is certain to be invited to attend so that he can put his view and take part in any discussion. He can ask permission to attend should any item down for discussion be of special concern to his department. And by reading the minutes he will know the decisions reached on all matters that came up at Cabinet and can administer his department accordingly. But he misses the opportunity to decide upon issues not of concern to his department.

CABINET COMMITTEES

Cabinet Committees are not new; indeed the idea of asking a

few Ministers to look at a special problem is probably as old as the idea of the Cabinet. But increasingly in recent years all the evidence points to a greater use not only of *ad hoc* committees but also of standing committees to which a particular and continuing field of Government affairs is assigned.

A formal system of this kind first came into prominence during the war of 1914-18, particularly during Mr. Lloyd George's War Cabinet of 1916-19, but the establishment of the Committee of Imperial Defence in May 1904 was the first major development in this direction. And the Committee of Imperial Defence was a reconstitution of the Defence Committee of the Cabinet, originally established by Lord Salisbury in 1895. The Prime Minister was usually the Chairman and the Committee of Imperial Defence usually contained all the Ministers directly concerned with military questions, and the Chiefs of Staff. The detailed work was entrusted to a network of sub-committees, while the main Committee laid down the broad lines of policy, and also acted as a clearing house and if necessary as a court of appeal. The Committee was advisory, decisions still remaining with the Cabinet and execution with the departments. As the character of warfare became more total, so the sub-committees extended to cover manpower and industry. Early in 1939 the organisation of this side of the Cabinet's activities was as follows:

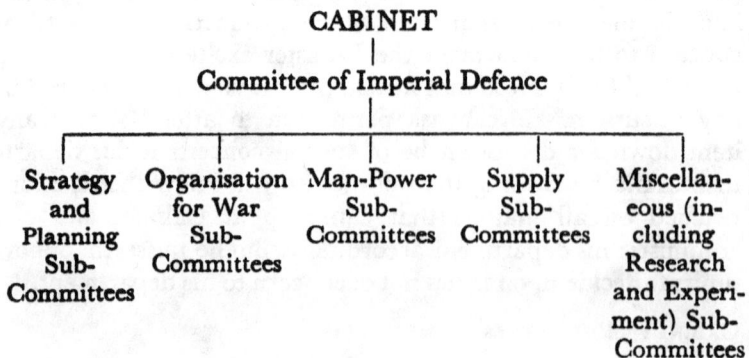

CABINET
|
Committee of Imperial Defence
|

Strategy and Planning Sub-Committees	Organisation for War Sub-Committees	Man-Power Sub-Committees	Supply Sub-Committees	Miscellaneous (including Research and Experiment) Sub-Committees

The sub-committees are shown in groups and the title for each group covers a variety of standing and *ad hoc* sub-committees. In the Strategical and Planning Group the most important was the Chiefs of Staff Sub-Committee of which the Prime Minister was Chairman though he did not always preside, for at that time there was also a Minister for Co-ordination of Defence. The Chiefs of Staffs' Sub-Committee had a most important sub-committee concerned with Joint Planning. Included in the Organization for War group was the long established Oversea Defence Committee and the two newly created Civil Defence Sub-Committees. The main committees included in the Supply group were the Principal Supply Officers Committee (which had a vast organization working under it), the Food Supply Committee and the Oil Board.[1]

On the purely civil side of the Cabinet no such permanent committee system developed. Many committees were established during the period 1914-18, but they did not continue into the post-war period either because they had been set up for a particular function which they had discharged, as was the Home Rule Bill Committee, or because it was thought preferable that the matter should be dealt with by the Cabinet once it had returned to its normal full size. The only exception was the Home Affairs Committee originally established in June 1918. As originally constituted its procedure and scope were as follows:[2]

(1) A Standing Cabinet Committee of Home Affairs to consider all questions of internal policy;

(2) The Committee should meet regularly once a week at a fixed hour;

(3) It should be the duty of the Committee to consider all domestic questions which require the co-operation of more than one Department, or of such importance that they would otherwise call for the consideration of the Cabinet. The Committee should have a wide discretion in dealing finally

[1] *Royal United Services Institution Journal*, May 1939: "The Machinery of the Committee of Imperial Defence," Major-General H. L. Ismay.
[2] Addison: *Four and a Half Years*, Vol. II, p. 542.

with questions on which agreement is reached, and should
refer to the War Cabinet only such large questions of policy as
require Cabinet sanction, or questions on which they have
been unable to reach agreement;

(4) The Secretary to the War Cabinet should have instructions to
refer to the Committee all questions falling within their
competence before they are brought to the Cabinet, unless
there are special reasons of urgency which make this course
impossible, and that the Secretary of the Committee should be
a Member of the War Cabinet Secretariat;

(5) The Chairman should have authority to invite the attendance
of other Ministers as occasion might require and those
Ministers should be authorised to seek the assistance of the
Committee where they feel the need for it.

The Home Secretary was in the Chair and the other members
were the Presidents of the Board of Trade, of the Local Government Board, and of the Board of Education, the Ministers of
Reconstruction and of Labour, the Secretary of State for Scotland and one of the Law Officers of the Crown.

Though according to Jennings[1] writing in 1935 the Committee had been reconstituted by every Cabinet it does not
appear to have fulfilled its original intention of considering
"all questions of internal policy," but to have become in effect a
kind of Legislation Committee. In this capacity during the inter-
war period it dealt with the drafting of Government Bills and
with the planning of the legislative work of the session, but not
sufficient is known publicly to be able to say whether it operated
as a real home affairs committee on any scale. It was to be
expected that a system found convenient when the Cabinet
was composed of only six Ministers and with its attention
almost wholly on waging a major war should not continue in
the same form when the Cabinet contained some 20 Ministers
most of whom were concerned with home affairs. Nevertheless
it is clear that the Cabinet found it useful to have a Standing
Committee which concerned itself with drafts of Bills and with
the legislative programme.

Mention should be made of the Economic Advisory Council

[1]*Cabinet Government*, p. 199.

established by Mr. Ramsay MacDonald in January 1930. Though the Council reported to the Cabinet and had the Prime Minister as chairman it was as its name implies an advisory body and not a sub-committee of the Cabinet. It contained a high proportion of outside experts and mainly worked through two standing committees—on Economic Information and on Scientific Research—which were even more like the advisory bodies found in departments. The Council ceased to play any significant part after the Labour Government went out of office in 1931, but remained in being.[1]

At the outbreak of war, in September 1939, Mr. Neville Chamberlain established a War Cabinet of nine members in which was merged the Committee of Imperial Defence. There were four main groups of Cabinet committees: (1) military operations and intelligence; (2) home policy; (3) civil defence; and (4) priority questions. Very shortly afterwards, following public criticism, a Ministerial and an official Committee on Economic Policy were added.

When Mr. Churchill became Prime Minister in May 1940 he introduced a new system the main feature of which was that the Cabinet (of five members) became largely a committee of chairmen of committees and not of departmental Ministers. The structure was as follows:

Cabinet	Special Functions
Prime Minister and Minister of Defence	Assisted by a Defence Committee of the three Service Ministers with the Chiefs of Staffs as Advisers.
Lord President	Chairman of the Lord President's Committee to concert and direct the work of the five Ministerial Committees covering Economic and Home Affairs (Production Council, Economic Policy, Food Policy, Home Policy, and Civil Defence Committees) and to ensure that their work was properly co-ordinated and that no part of the field was left uncovered.

[1]Sir John Anderson: "The Organisation of Economic Studies in Relation to the Problems of Government" (Stamp Memorial Lecture, 1947), p. 12.

Lord Privy Seal	Chairman of the Food Policy Committee (dealing with problems of food including food production); and of the Home Policy Committee (dealing with questions relating to the home front and social services and responsible for framing of regulations and draft legislation).
Secretary of State for Foreign Affairs	Questions of Foreign Policy continued to be submitted by the Foreign Secretary direct to the War Cabinet.
Minister without Portfolio	Chairman of the Production Council (gave general directions as to the organisation and the priority of production for war purposes) and of the Economic Policy Committee (concerted and directed general economic policy).

This structure did not last very long. By October 1940 three Departmental Ministers had been brought into the War Cabinet. In January 1941 the important change was announced. As a result the policy of having a Cabinet consisting of non-departmental Ministers who acted as chairmen of committees was largely abandoned. The Cabinet of January 1941 was composed of the Prime Minister, Lord President, Lord Privy Seal, Foreign Secretary, Chancellor of the Exchequer, Minister without Portfolio, Minister of Labour and National Service and Minister of Aircraft Production (8 in all). The Production Council became the Production Executive under the chairmanship of the Minister of Labour and National Service who had entered the Cabinet late in 1940. The Economic Policy Committee ceased to exist, its general economic functions were transferred to the Lord President's Committee and its functions in respect of imports were transferred to an Import Executive under the chairmanship of the Minister of Supply who was not, however, a member of the War Cabinet.

Further changes took place in February 1942 following the

46

establishment of a Ministry of Production.[1] As a result of all this the Lord President's Committee emerged as the major Cabinet Committee. Most of the other committees had disappeared or had become in effect sub-committees. In the words of the Prime Minister speaking in February 1942; "The Lord President of the Council presides over what is, in certain aspects, almost a parallel Cabinet concerned with home affairs. . . . An immense mass of business is discharged at their frequent meetings, and it is only in the case of a serious difference or in very large questions that the War Cabinet as such is concerned."[2]

The developments which took place on the Defence side of the Cabinet's work centred on the personality and position of the Prime Minister. In 1936 there had been appointed a Minister for the Co-ordination of Defence, to assist the Prime Minister in the task of overseeing the rearmament programme, and this post remained until April 1940. Mr. Neville Chamberlain's War Cabinet of eight members contained this Minister in addition to the three Ministerial heads of the Service Departments. When Mr. Churchill became Prime Minister he assumed the additional title of Minister of Defence. It had become clear that only the Prime Minister was in the position to control the mobilisation and direction of the whole resources of the nation. The position of the Minister for the Co-ordination of Defence had been anomalous for some time before the post was abolished.

Though there was a Minister of Defence, no Ministry of Defence was created during the war, and

"The Minister of Defence operated by bringing together from the Service Departments and elsewhere those Ministers or officials who would be responsible for the execution of plans when approved. He used as his staff the small military Secretariat of the War Cabinet, which had previously served the Committee of Imperial Defence. The military head of the Secretariat became his chief Staff Officer and a member of the Chiefs of Staff Committee. The task of the Secretariat was to draft reports and telegrams on behalf of the Chiefs of Staff, to ensure co-ordination

[1] For the development during this period see *British War Economy* by W. K. Hancock and M. M. Gowing, pp. 216-223.
[2] H.C. Deb. 24th February, 1942, Col. 38.

and continuity in the activities of the various committees and sub-committees dealing with military questions, and generally to facilitate the smooth running of the inter-Service machine. It was not their duty to act as military advisers to the Minister of Defence. It was their duty to procure for him advice from those who would be responsible for action."[1]

There were two main Defence Committees—one for Operations and one for Supply. The Defence Committee (Operations)

"for the greater part of the war consisted of the Prime Minister and Minister of Defence (in the Chair), the Deputy Prime Minister, the Foreign Secretary, the Minister of Production, the Service Ministers and the Chiefs of Staff, other Ministers attending when matters affecting their departmental responsibilities were under consideration. This Committee examined the military plans prepared by the Chiefs of Staff and the Joint Staffs and took decisions on behalf of the War Cabinet. A parallel body, the Defence Committee (Supply), dealt with the main lines of the production programmes. The duties of the Prime Minister as Minister of Defence were never defined. It was left for Mr. Churchill to develop a method of working, through the Defence Committee and the Chiefs of Staff Committee, which enabled him to provide the drive without which successful warlike operations cannot be conducted."[2]

CHANGES AFTER AUGUST, 1945.

This kind of arrangement was continued by Mr. Attlee for about a year after the end of the war, but in October 1946 a separate Minister of Defence was appointed. The form of the new organisation was summarised by the White Paper on the Central Organisation for Defence in the following manner:[3]

"(a) The Prime Minister will retain the supreme responsibility for defence.

(b) The Defence Committee, under the Chairmanship of the Prime Minister, will take over the functions of the old Committee of Imperial Defence, and will be responsible to the Cabinet both for the review of current strategy and for co-ordinating departmental action in preparation for war.

[1] Central Organisation for Defence. Cmd. 6923 (October 1946), p. 4.
[2] Ibid, p. 3.
[3] Ibid., p. 6.

(c) A new post of Minister of Defence, with a Ministry, will be created. The Minister of Defence will be responsible to Parliament for certain subjects, which are defined in paragraph 26 (see below), affecting the three Services and their supply. In addition, he will be Deputy Chairman of the Defence Committee; and he will also preside over meetings with the Chiefs of Staff whenever he or they may so desire.

(d) The Chiefs of Staff Committee will remain responsible for preparing strategic appreciations and military plans, and for submitting them to the Defence Committee; and the Joint Staff system will be retained and developed under their direction.

(e) The Service Ministers will continue to be responsible to Parliament for the administration of their Services in accordance with the general policy approved by the Cabinet and within the resources allotted to them."

It is clear that the Minister of Defence is envisaged as a kind of super-departmental Minister, rather like the Minister of Production during the war, and not as was the Lord President of the Council during that period. His functions are:

"(a) The apportionment, in broad outline, of available resources between the three Services in accordance with the strategic policy laid down by the Defence Committee. This will include the framing of general policy to govern research and development, and the correlation of production programmes.

(b) The settlement of questions of general administration on which a common policy for the three Services is desirable.

(c) The administration of inter-Service organisations, such as Combined Operations Headquarters and the Joint Intelligence Bureau."[1]

On the question of the Minister's staff, the White Paper said that for the discharge of the above three functions he should not need a large staff.

"He will have as his principal advisers a Permanent Secretary, a Chief Staff Officer, the Chairman of the Joint War Production

[1] *Ibid.*, p. 7.

D

Staff and the Chairman of the Committee on Defence Research Policy. These will be assisted by a relatively small staff, partly civil and partly military, which among their other duties will provide the Secretariat for the Committees and Joint Staffs through which the Minister will mainly work. The civil members of this staff will be drawn from the Civil Service in the normal way. The military members will be seconded from the three Services as are the military officers of the Cabinet Secretariat."[1]

Even so the staff is larger than just a secretariat, for the Minister assumed control over certain existing inter-Service organisations—e.g. Combined Operations Headquarters and the Imperial Defence College.

On the supply side of defence there is a Ministerial Production Committee, consisting of the Service Ministers and the Ministers of Supply and Labour with the Minister of Defence in the Chair. Working for this committee there is a Joint War Production Staff composed of serving officers and officials from the service and civil departments concerned.

When Mr. Attlee's administration took office in August 1945 the President of the Board of Trade took over the functions of the Minister of Production and for a time held both titles, before the latter was abolished. The Lord President and his committee retained a dominating position in the central machinery. The pressure of the economic situation, however, caused two Ministerial committees concerned with economic policy to be established: one, with the Lord President in the Chair, was concerned with internal policy, and the other, with the Prime Minister in the Chair, dealt with overseas policy. This rather strange dichotomy continued until the appointment on September 29th, 1947, of Sir Stafford Cripps as Minister for Economic Affairs.[2] The two committees were then merged into a single Ministerial Economic Policy Committee concerned with the whole range of the country's economic affairs, with the Prime Minister as chairman, the Minister for Economic Affairs acting if the Prime Minister could not attend. Apparently membership of this committee is confined to a small number of

[1] *Ibid.*, p. 10.
[2] See *The Times*, 30th September, 1947.

senior Ministers, and concentrates on major issues of economic policy. Under it, however, and concerned with day-to-day matters, a committee composed of the departmental Ministers directly concerned was established with the Minister for Economic Affairs in the Chair. The new Minister had no Ministry in the normal sense of the term, but had a small personal staff and the services of the Central Economic Planning Staff, the Economic Information Unit and the Economic Section of the Cabinet Secretariat. On November 13th of the same year, upon Mr. Dalton's resignation, Sir Stafford Cripps became the Chancellor of the Exchequer and took with him the functions he had as Minister for Economic Affairs, but abandoned the title. Thus by chance the problem of the relations between the Treasury and the Minister for Economic Affairs was settled within a comparatively short time. The Committee arrangement continued, Sir Stafford Cripps retaining the chairmanship of the Committee of Departmental Ministers concerned with production and continuing as member of the small Economic Policy Committee.

The Lord President of the Council, besides continuing as Leader of the House of Commons, continued to be the Minister concerned with co-ordinating such matters as the Government's legislative programme and the social services.

CONCLUSIONS

It would be unwise to generalise too much on the basis of the exceptional circumstances of the War and of the immediate post-war period. But there are reasons for believing that a system of standing Cabinet committees is now well accepted and that indeed a formal pattern is beginning to emerge. The pattern chosen at any one time must necessarily depend upon the personalities of the Prime Minister and of his senior colleagues. The basis of the pattern, however, would be an attempted grouping of subjects according to three or four main fields of Government activity. The most obvious grouping is external affairs, defence, and internal affairs with a possible sub-division of the latter into production and economic affairs and other home front questions. The Foreign Secretary would normally be the leader in external affairs (which would include Commonwealth affairs) but this is a side of Government policy with which the Prime Minister has traditionally been closely associated. The Minister of Defence is obviously designed for the co-ordination of defence policy, though here again the Prime Minister, particularly in times of crisis, has normally taken the lead. On internal affairs there is the possibility of a division of the field between the Chancellor of the Exchequer and the Lord President of the Council. Alternatively the Chancellor might be left as a purely departmental Minister and the co-ordination of economic affairs be with the Lord President or with some other holder of an ancient office (e.g. Lord Privy Seal) or a specially designated Minister (e.g. Minister for Economic Affairs) might be appointed.

Under such a system, which is rather like the present arrangements, there would clearly be a special and closer relationship between the Prime Minister and the Ministers charged with the co-ordinating duties than that existing between the Prime Minister and other Ministers, even if these Ministers are in the Cabinet. The term "inner cabinet" is not much liked and indeed it would not represent the true constitutional position. But there would be likely to grow up informal or formal arrangements whereby these senior Ministers met from time to time and discussed common problems and general policy, so keeping in step with one another. What would be the long run effect of that on Cabinet meetings is difficult to prophesy. In one sense, however, it would be nothing more than a formal recognition of a situation which has obtained for many years. In any Cabinet, with or without a system of committees, there are always two or three, little less powerful than the Prime Minister, whose views he would wish to have and who by virtue of personal ability or party position are recognised as being more important than their fellow Ministers.

Mr. Francis Williams[1] is inclined to claim that Mr. Attlee's Cabinet system is a revolution in the structure of the Cabinet. He refers to an "alteration in the traditional pattern of British Cabinet Government" and explains "For a Cabinet of equal

[1] *The Triple Challenge.* Chapter Five—"The New Pattern of Government."

departmental Ministers under a Prime Minister who is himself 'the first among equals' there has been substituted a pyramidical pattern of government designed to secure greater rapidity in action and a tighter centralised control of general political strategy." In a book which is frankly whole-hearted in support of the Labour Government it was perhaps to be expected that Mr. Williams should claim that Mr. Attlee had revolutionised the structure of the Cabinet, instead of his having adapted a committee system already in existence. Nevertheless there is this very important distinguishing feature of Mr. Attlee's Cabinet structure: standing committees are being used in the field of non-military affairs even though the Cabinet has returned to almost its normal size. Some such system of committees has to be used when the Cabinet is composed of only six or eight Ministers, as was the War Cabinet, and when this body is concentrating the major part of its attention on military matters. But perhaps this is only a difference of degree, for as we have already seen the Cabinet of 1949, though of seventeen members, nevertheless left out some fourteen Ministerial heads of departments. In these circumstances also it is necessary to devise a means for bringing such Ministers into discussions with their colleagues. As most of the excluded Ministers are concerned with industry and production it is clearly very convenient to have a committee concerned with planning production of which they are members. Similarly the Defence Committee is likely to be the method whereby the three Service Ministers, excluded from the Cabinet, are brought into discussions of Defence Policy.

Thus it comes about, as Mr. Williams points out, that there is a kind of hierarchy of Ministers. The Prime Minister and his three senior colleagues—Lord President of the Council, Foreign Secretary and Chancellor of the Exchequer—take general responsibility for one or other of the main fields of Government activity;[1] the other Ministers who are in the Cabinet and who therefore partake of collective responsibility as well as each being responsible to Parliament for his own department; and the

[1] The Minister of Defence is in a kind of intermediate position, according to Mr. Williams.

53

Ministerial heads who are excluded and are brought only into such Cabinet discussions as are of particular relevance to them. The whole is knit together by the secretarial facilities provided by the Cabinet Secretariat and by a system of committees.

Experience may show that Mr. Attlee has struck the happy mean between those who urge the merits of a small policy-making Cabinet and those who would prefer to see all Ministers in the Cabinet. It would not be impossible to reduce the number of departments, for example by merging the Ministry of Civil Aviation with the Ministry of Transport, but it is not easy to see ten or so Ministries disappearing. One or two of the non-departmental Ministerial posts, for example Lord Privy Seal, could be abolished or left out of the Cabinet, but it is obviously useful for the Prime Minister to have a few such Ministers readily available for special jobs. Altogether then it is unlikely that the size of the Cabinet can be kept below twenty without leaving outside quite a number of Ministers.

Mr. Amery has said he would have "a Cabinet of half a dozen, all entirely free from ordinary departmental duties. This Cabinet would deal with current administrative questions, ..., by bringing into its discussions the departmental Ministers directly affected . . . it should also have regular meetings set aside for the discussion of future policy . . . (its work) would be expedited by standing and *ad hoc* committees . . . over which members of the Cabinet would preside with the advantage both of their higher authority and of their freedom from other routine work."[1] The idea of a very small Cabinet of non-departmental supervising Ministers has received support at various times, particularly during the two world wars. It is indeed very similar to the short-lived scheme introduced by Mr. Churchill[2] in May 1940. It is doubtful, however, whether

[1] *Thoughts on the Constitution* (1947), pp. 90-91.
[2] Mr. Churchill did not believe in a small Cabinet of Ministers without Departmental duties, he preferred to call together Ministers with definite executive responsibilities. See *The Gathering Storm*, p. 320, for his attitude in 1939 when offered the Admiralty—"I naturally preferred a definite task to that exalted brooding over the work done by others which may well be the lot of a Minister, however influential, who has no department. It is easier to give directions than advice, and more agreeable to have the right to act, even in a limited sphere, than the privilege to talk at large." For his views on the experiment of 1940 see H.C. Deb., Vol. 368, Cols 256-265 (22nd January, 1941).

it would ever be a workable system save in very exceptional circumstances. For one thing, it is doubtful whether any six Ministers would ever be found willing and able to bear the whole responsibility of Government for any length of time, particularly having regard to the tremendous range of Government activity these days. Moreover, it is unlikely that such a small Cabinet would accord for long with political realities. There would always be a number of able and ambitious Ministers with support in the Party whose views on matters outside the responsibilities of their departments would have to be taken into account if the Prime Minister and the Cabinet were to maintain the solidarity of the Party. Again the distinction talked of by Mr. Amery between policy and administration, though attractive in theory, is illusive in practice. At almost every stage in the discussion of major issues of policy these supervising Ministers would require the views and advice of the departments actually administering the services concerned. Either only the supervising Minister directly concerned would hear such views and advice, in which case it is difficult to see on what the other five Ministers in the Cabinet would base their decision, or else all six would hear them, in which case, this is how the Cabinet normally works. For these and other reasons it will probably always be found desirable to have a larger Cabinet than six and to include in it some of the leading departmental Ministers. Mr. Attlee's Cabinet at the end of 1949, composed of seventeen members, though larger than the ten or twelve mentioned by the Haldane Committee on the Machinery of Government, is probably very near the size which balances the advantages and disadvantages of the two extremes.[1]

[1]For the authoritative views of Sir John Anderson, see his Romanes Lecture, "The Machinery of Government," 1946. *Public Administration.* Vol. xxiv. pp. 147-156.

CHAPTER III

THE STRUCTURE OF
CENTRAL ADMINISTRATION

by PROFESSOR W. J. M. MACKENZIE, M.A., LL.B.

IN matters of Government the English have generally been more
theoretical than they care to admit. Burke impressed upon them
that it was in this absence of theory that they excelled the
French: yet it is to England, not to France, that we owe such
subtle formulations as those of limited monarchy, the separation
and interaction of powers, Cabinet responsibility, Dominion
status. The theory of Crown and Parliament has been elabor-
rated in detail: there has been much discussion of the structure
of the Cabinet and of its co-ordinating function. Yet there has
been little discussion, political or academic, of what it is to co-
ordinate. In the thirty years which have elapsed since the
Haldane Committee reported[1] little has been said or written about
the Committee's theory of the allocation of functions between
British Government departments, and the only competing
theory (if it can be called a theory) is the view that this is a
subject on which generalisation would be unwise and perhaps
improper. In Britain departmental organisation (it is said) is a
matter almost entirely within the discretion of the Crown; or
(to put it less abstractly) the Minister who is responsible for
the formulation and execution of policy is given a free hand
to shape his instrument, so that his responsibility may be
unmistakable and unimpaired.[2] With this happy freedom is

---

[1] Cd.9230 of 1918: There is a useful contemporary commentary in Ministry of
Reconstruction Pamphlet No. 38 : "The Business of Government." It is rumoured
that a Cabinet Committee on the Machinery of Government existed during the
Second World War, but no hint of its conclusions has reached the public : *cf.* however, Sir Edward Bridges' evidence before the Estimates Committee (H.C.143 of
1946/47, p. 100) : "We have had in the Treasury for some years past now a quite
small section of two or three people working on what one might call the higher level
machinery   government questions, with a group of high officials which, in turn,
has worked with a Ministerial Committee."

[2] *cf.* Sir Edward Bridges' evidence, p. 102: "Of course, if you look at the strict
constitutional doctrine, there is no doubt that the Permanent Secretary of a
department is responsible to the Minister for the efficient organisation of the
department."

contrasted the misery of Washington where almost all executive agencies are created and regulated by Congress, so that the responsibility of Cabinet Ministers and even that of the President is lost in a maze of semi-independent commissions and agencies and bureaux, each constituting an autonomous Parliamentary "interest" or "lobby."

This has an attractive air. It appears to exclude bureaucracy and to put responsibility on one man who can be attacked and if necessary dismissed. But surely we must now sadly admit that it is false, as the separation of powers between Crown and Parliament had become false in Bagehot's day? In modern conditions no political programme can become a policy until it has been shaped by an existing body of expert departmental opinion: and policies are too large and too urgent for new agencies to be tailored in each case to fit the figure of the individual Minister. Even if a new Ministry is to be created it must be built round an existing nucleus of departmental experience: it has been rare to attempt any other plan, and where it has been attempted it has been followed generally by a period of waste and confusion in which the original conception has been lost.[1]

We can, therefore, no longer take refuge in personalities: whether we like it or not, the subject must be accepted as one of constitutional importance, and some attempt must be made to formulate general principles. This does not mean that plain and unalterable rules of administrative organisation are somewhere to be found: merely that we cannot criticise institutions except by engaging in a search for principle.

1. THE HALDANE REPORT

This search must begin with some consideration of the Haldane Report, which has for a generation of administrative reformers assumed the status almost of holy writ. Little is known yet about its compilation except from internal evidence; but it is pretty safe to conjecture that it was largely the work of these three artists in influence, Lord Haldane, Sir Robert Morant,

[1]The Ministry of Information is the classic instance of this.

and Mrs. Webb; that they were well aware that they spoke only for a tiny fraction of public opinion; and that they were deeply concerned to promote by stealth certain objects very close to their hearts—in particular generous provision for research, the efficiency of the legal system, the creation of a true Ministry of Health, the proper utilisation of the industrial labour force, the break-up of the Poor Law. These objects are linked and harmonised in their Report by the great principle that the functions of Government should be organised according to the service to be rendered, not according to the clients to be served. It is easy to see that the principle is demonstrated only by generalisation from one instance, that of their own child, the Board of Education; that it is introduced mainly to justify by deduction their dream-children, a Ministry of Research, a Ministry of Justice, a Ministry of Employment, and a true Ministry of Health; and that it is essentially a quiet reassertion of the theories of administration expressed by the Webbs in the Minority Report on the Poor Law in 1909. Its origin is thus more historical than scientific, but it is none the less a great principle—the first principle ever enunciated on the subject in England.

In addition to this explicit principle, the Haldane Report contains two important concealed assumptions. One of these is that a series of great bureaucratic departments already exists in Whitehall: the correct deployment of the available civil servants is everything, the personal influence of the Minister is insignificant. It is perhaps not easy now to appreciate that it was a new thought in 1918 outside the circle of "benevolent despots" to which the authors of the Report belonged. But throughout the nineteenth century the academic theory of the constitution had regarded the high places of Government as "offices"—bundles of legal powers to be exercised in turn by individual politicians; not as "departments," organisations of experts pursuing their own altruistic but implacable course. It is not until 1908, in the works of Graham Wallas and A. L. Lowell, that bureaucracy begins to find its place in the books,[1] and it becomes

[1] *Human Nature in Politics* Part II, Chap. III, *The Government of England*, Vol. I, Chap. IV-VIII. The "Departments" are clearly regarded as "offices" in H. D.

official only in 1920 in the grandiloquent phrase "the Departments of the Public Service" used by the civil servants themselves in the Report of the Whitley Council Committee of that year.[1]

The second assumption is more questionable. "The main functions of the Cabinet" says the Report, are:[2]

"(a) the final determination of the policy to be submitted to Parliament;

(b) the supreme control of the national executive in accordance with the policy prescribed by Parliament; and

(c) the continuous co-ordination and delimitation of the activities of the several Departments of State."

This is so blandly stated that its enormity at first sight escapes notice. What? No reference *at all* to the fact that these men are first and foremost party leaders? that the Cabinet is historically a cabal of politicians who must hang together, lest they hang separately? that in constitutional theory its primary role is to keep the vessel on some steady course amid the high seas of public clamour and political intrigue? The committee's assumption here is that the machinery of Government can in the twentieth century be studied apart from the politics of Government; that such a study will suggest improvements of the highest order of importance; and that these improvements can in some sense be carried through "outside politics." Did they seriously believe that there can be anything of first-rate importance in Government which is not politically important?

Traill's *Central Government* (1st ed. 1881): they are almost neglected in Hearn's *The Government of England* (1st ed. 1867, 2nd ed. 1887): in Leonard Courtney's *The Working Constitution of the U.K.* (1901), and in Sidney Low's *The Governance of England* (1904). In 1912 W. S. McKechnie can still speak of an "Oligarchy of Officials" when he means an oligarchy of Cabinet Ministers (*The New Democracy and the Constitution*, p. 23). R. H. Gretton (*The King's Government*, 1913) is (like Lowell) the forerunner of a new age. Yet G. W. E. Russell (who knew what he was talking about) is reputed to have said in 1909 "the permanent Civil Service whose chiefs have been, at least since the days of Bagehot, recognised as the real rulers of the country." (*Ministry of Reconstruction Pamphlet No.* 38, Pt. III, p. 5.)

[1]Civil Service National Whitley Council: "Report of Joint Committee on the Organisation of the Civil Service, 1921," Para. 43.

[2]p. 5.

Or is this merely the well-worn trick of the committee-man who slips through his proposals by depreciating their significance and smothering it in technicalities?

To these three principles, the Committee adds an analysis under ten headings of the main functions of the State. It will be convenient first to summarise briefly what has happened since 1918 to the departmental organisation of British government; to consider then what light this development throws on the functional division suggested by the Haldane Committee; and to return finally to the larger generalisations from which they proceeded.

2. HISTORICAL SUMMARY

A detailed history is naturally impossible here, but a bare outline may be of some value for reference:

In 1914 the main departments were :—[1]

> The Lord Chancellor's Department.
> The Treasury.
> Home Office (Secretary of State).
> Foreign Office (Secretary of State).
> Colonial Office (Secretary of State).
> War Office (Secretary of State).
> India Office (Secretary of State).
> Scottish Office (Secretary).
> Irish Office (Chief Secretary).
> Admiralty.
> Board of Trade.
> Local Government Board.
> Board of Agriculture and Fisheries.
> Board of Education.
> Post Office.
> Office of Works.

To these were added during the first World War the following·—

> Air Ministry (Secretary of State).
> Ministry of Munitions.
> Directorate of National Service.

[1]It is interesting to note that no " Ministry " existed by that name before the first World War.

Ministry of Labour.
Ministry of Pensions.
Ministry of Reconstruction.
Ministry of Blockade.
Office of the Food Controller.
Office of the Shipping Controller.
Ministry of Propaganda (Chancellor of the Duchy of
    Lancaster).
Mines Department (Under-Secretary).
Department of Overseas Trade (Under-Secretary).
Department of Scientific and Industrial Research (Lord
    President of the Council).

Out of these additions there survived in the early 1920's only
the Air Ministry (which now included the Civil Aviation Dept.
and the Meteorological Office), the Ministry of Labour, the
Ministry of Pensions, and the D.S.I.R., as well as the two
sub-departments, Overseas Trade and Mines. The Chief
Secretary for Ireland had vanished; the Board of Agriculture
had become a Ministry, the Local Government Board had
added somewhat to its functions, but still scarcely deserved its
new name, Ministry of Health. A Ministry of Transport had,
however, been constructed out of the Railway Dept. of the
Board of Trade, and it had also taken over responsibility for
electricity.

The period between the wars changed little. It is necessary
to record only that the Dominions office was budded off from
the Colonial Office in 1925, that the Secretary for Scotland
became a Secretary of State in 1926, and that two phantoms
without departments appeared briefly as Minister for League
of Nation Affairs and as Minister for the Co-ordination of
Defence. But a new period begins with the act creating the
Ministry of Supply, which received the Royal Assent on 13th
July, 1939. The tide then rose higher than in 1914-1918 and
it has receded less. During the war of 1939 there were added:—

Ministry of Defence (directed by the Prime Minister).
Ministry of Production.
Ministry of Home Security.

Ministry of Economic Warfare.
Ministry of Food.
Ministry of Information.
Ministry of Aircraft Production.
Ministry of Civil Aviation.
Ministry of Town and Country Planning.
Ministry of Reconstruction.

In addition the Ministry of Labour became also the Ministry of National Service; a Ministry of Fuel and Power was constructed round the nucleus of the Mines Department; the Office of Works burgeoned out as Ministry of Works and Buildings (after a brief interlude as Works and Planning); the Ministry of Transport became War Transport, with the accession of shipping from the Board of Trade and the loss of electricity to the Ministry of Fuel and Power. There were also at various times a Cabinet Minister resident in Washington as Ambassador, and four other Ministers *in partibus*, in West Africa, the Mediterranean, the Middle East, and Washington (for Supply); this experiment does not concern us here, nor does the invention of the titular office of Minister of State.

Since the war there have vanished utterly only the Ministry of Economic Warfare and the Ministry of Reconstruction among the new Ministries, the India Office and the Department of Overseas Trade among the old. The Ministry of Production re-emerged briefly as the Ministry of Economic Affairs, and then vanished into the Treasury: the Ministry of Defence has been formally constituted under its own Minister. Home Security and Aircraft Production have been attached to the Home Office and the Ministry of Supply respectively: the Ministry of Information has been reduced to a "Central Office" under the Lord President. Other changes have been minor and titular: the Board of Education has become a Ministry (an odd piece of departmental psychology), the Dominions Office has as a matter of diplomacy become the Commonwealth Relations Office.

3. THE HALDANE DIVISIONS

Let us now plot the result of these changes against the

analysis of functions proposed by the Haldane Committee, giving credit for double appearances as necessary. There is of course nothing authoritative about this: probably no two observers would agree exactly on these groupings.

    I.   *Finance:* Treasury.

    II. *National Defence:*
> Ministry of Defence.
> Admiralty.
> War Office.
> Air Ministry.
> Home Office (Home Security).
> Ministry of Supply.
> Ministry of Pensions.

    III. *External Affairs:*
> Foreign Office (including its German Section and the British Council, which are independently organised).
> Office of Commonwealth Relations.
> Colonial Office.

    IV. *Research and Information:*[1]
> D.S.I.R. and almost all other Departments.

    V. *Production, Transport and Commerce:*
> Treasury.
> Board of Trade.
> Ministry of Supply.
> Ministry of Food.
> Ministry of Works and Buildings.
> Ministry of Agriculture.
> Ministry of Transport.
> Ministry of Civil Aviation.
> Ministry of Fuel and Power.
> Post Office.
> Ministry of Health (Housing Programme).
> Ministry of Labour and National Service.
> Colonial Office.
> D.S.I.R.

[1]The C.O.I. does not belong here, as the Haldane Report uses the word "Information" in a different sense: it means for them the information of Ministers, not the information of the public.

VI. *Employment:*
>> Ministry of Labour and National Service.
>> Ministry of Transport (Mercantile Marine).

VII. *Supplies:* (i.e. Government purchases).
>> The same list as under V.

VIII. *Education:*
>> Treasury (Universities).
>> Ministry of Agriculture (Universities).
>> D.S.I.R. (Universities).
>> Ministry of Education.

IX. *Health:*
>> Ministry of Health.
>> Ministry of Food.
>> Ministry of Education.
>> Ministry of Labour (Factory Inspection).

X. *Justice:*
>> Home Office.
>> Lord Chancellor's Department.
>> Lord Chief Justice.

It will be noticed that there are certain omissions.

(a) *The Scottish Office*, if it were included, would appear under at least seven of the ten headings, as it is excluded only from External Affairs and National Finance, and in part from Employment; this is an untidy arrangement, but one cannot set bounds to the march of a department in such circumstances. For Scotland is unconsciously playing Parnell's game by different means: in the 1945 election the balance between the parties was more even in Scotland than anywhere else in the country,[1] and a small dose of nationalism in the scales can easily tip the balance either way. A Welsh Office would probably exist by this time, were it not that Wales disposes of fewer seats and is almost hopeless ground for the Conservative Opposition.[2]

[1] 40 supporters of the Labour Government: 32 of the Opposition: 1 *bona fide* Independent: 1 Communist.
[2] In 1945: 25 Lab., 7 Lib, 4 Con. and Lib. Nat. The Conservative programme for Wales (1949) still refuses a Welsh Office and a Minister exclusively concerned with Welsh affairs.

(b) *The Ministry of National Insurance*, on the other hand, is at first sight a very elegant instance of the "Haldane principle." It appears to perform a single service, the distribution (directly or indirectly) of all cash benefits except war pensions, and its work is governed by a reasonably modern and comprehensive code of statutes and regulations. Yet the Ministry fits none of the Haldane categories, and its work (if it is to be well done) will ramify into every department of the social services. It is better justified on the principle which the Haldane Committee rejects: its local offices may form central points of reference to which clients of the social services in the first instance will go for guidance. This holds out the prospect of an immense saving of time and temper for the public, but it can be realised only if the officials do better than the Haldane ideal of the "development of specialised capacity".[1] The Permanent Secretary, the girls at the counter, and most of those in between, will require general knowledge and sympathies as well as specialised technique.

(c) *The Ministry of Town and Country Planning* poses the same problem in a much less promising form. This appears at first sight to be master of a single specialist service, organised on a national scale and governed by a single code of statutes and statutory instruments. But in practice the experiment of planning land utilisation will not work unless the experts understand everyone else's business almost as well as they do their own. There are, of course, certain special skills involved, but the main problem is one of adjusting priorities between competing interests of great social, economic and political weight. The Ministry must attempt to adjudicate with authority between the demands of defence, industry, agriculture and amenity: and unless it succeeds we shall obtain only a series of short-lived local truces, not a national plan.[2]

Three of the Haldane divisions can be dealt with fairly simply:

[1] Report, Part I, Para 20.
[2] This aspect of the matter is fully appreciated by the Ministry: see Dame Evelyn Sharp's lecture on "Town & Country Planning" in *Public Admin.*, Vol. 26, p. 19.

Finance: Whatever else *the Treasury* may be, it is certainly a finance ministry of exceptional competence.

Employment: The work of a Ministry of Employment has now been concentrated more fully in the hands of *the Ministry of Labour* by the transfer to it of the administration of the Factory Acts; and one result of the experience of the Directorate of National Service in the 1914-18 war (a particularly painful experience for Mr. Neville Chamberlain) was that as Prime Minister he concentrated in one department the responsibility for finding manpower for the armed forces as well as for civil employment.

Education is now also intelligibly organised, at least up to school-leaving age, subject to certain minor difficulties as regards the health and feeding of children. Higher education is another matter. The titular master of the Universities is the Treasury, acting principally through the agency of the University Grants Committee, and providing some 58 per cent. of their total income.[1] But the ordinary University administrator is concerned very little with the Treasury, and not much with the U.G.C., though his livelihood depends on them. The main bulk of his official dealings (and they are endless) is with other bodies—the Ministry of Education and the corresponding departments in Scotland and Northern Ireland, the Ministry of Agriculture, the D.S.I.R., the Admiralty, the Ministry of Supply, the British Council, the Colonial Office, the Ministry of Labour (Joint Recruiting Boards), and the Civil Service Commission. This jumble of departments controls the flow of students, the provision of jobs for graduates, and the finance of research, and between them they settle the policy of the Universities and of other bodies responsible for higher education. Or rather there are left in the interstices of inter-departmental confusion large spaces in which the Universities can still make their own policy, even though they are now financially dependent on the State; academic freedom depends in part on inefficiency in the machinery of Government. We shall meet this point again elsewhere: inefficiency (which we deplore

[1] University Grants Committee Returns for the Academic Year 1947-48, p 5.

66

in theory) is sometimes to be treasured in practice, as a safe-guard against the gentle unthinking urge towards centralisation. "Separation of powers" is a doctrine which has some place in the theory of departmental organisation.

The other Haldane divisions all present more difficult problems which are not much nearer solution than they were thirty years ago.

4. DEFENCE

Here the three services have made steady and admirable progress. This is not only the result of bitter experience: from the Hartington Commission of 1890[1] to the White Paper on "Central Organisation for Defence,"[2] both soldiers and civilians have looked ahead with considerable acumen and persistence. The Ministry of Defence organisation has one theoretical flaw which it could not well avoid. A "co-ordinating" Ministry is always placed between opposite perils: it may either expand its own staff and duplicate the work of the departments to be co-ordinated, in order to be sure that it is well done: or it may remain small and remain at the mercy of its nominal subordinates. On the other hand, the three service departments constitute a relatively small and compact "parish," and the Ministry of Defence possesses an exceptionally experienced and able staff, which can be readily renewed through the Imperial Defence College, the Joint Planning Committee and other well-established inter-service bodies. If the way round this problem can be found, the Ministry is in a good position to find it.

Unfortunately the most anxious problems of defence now extend far beyond the scope of the new Ministry. *In the first place*, there is that of research and production for the services in time of peace. The Admiralty alone has been strong enough to retain substantial control over the design and production of its own weapons, but even its control does not extend to one of the most important naval weapons, the carrier-borne aeroplane. This, with all other problems of weapon research, weapon

[1]C.5979.
[2]Cmd.6923 of October 1946.

design, and weapon production, is the business of the Ministry of Supply; a Ministry which is stiff with "brass hats" and moves in a haze of military co-ordinating committees, but for all that an independent Ministry co-ordinate with the service departments, and directed (so far as it is directed at all) not by the Ministry of Defence but by the Ministry of Economic Affairs— in fact by the Treasury. This situation represents a temporary truce between nicely-balanced arguments and pressures. On the one hand it is said that military supplies are useless unless they are fit for fighting men to use, and unless they can be modified with extreme rapidity to meet changing tactical situations, and that these two points can only be secured if fighting men are given direct control at all stages.[1] On the other hand, it is said that the military mind is impervious to new ideas and blankly ignorant of the technique of production, so that it is dangerous to trust sailors, soldiers and airmen with any question affecting science or industry. These arguments are so sensible on both sides and so evenly balanced that no independent person would be shocked at the creation of a Ministry of War Supply free from service control. But the Ministry of Supply is very much more than that: it is also Ministry of Atomic Energy, Ministry of Iron and Steel and other metals, Ministry of Light Engineering, Ministry of Radio Engineering, Ministry of Aircraft Production, each of them a subject which deserves the individual attention of at least one eminent politician. In addition, through all these channels, the Ministry pours out a flood of money on research, which makes it the greatest single employer of scientists in Britain and perhaps in the world. What chance have the services to secure prompt hearing and resolute support amid this welter of competing civil interests?

In the second place, there is the problem of civil defence, which at present occupies the attention of only one department among the many which make up the Home Office. But civil defence is now the dominating issue in our strategic policy. It will be

[1]This side of the case has never been better argued than by Nigel Balchin's characterisation of a War Office arms expert, "Col. Holland," in *The Small Back Room*. The author was then Brigadier Balchin, Deputy Scientific Adviser to the Army Council.

madness (in some circumstances a noble madness, but still madness) to become involved in a major war unless we seriously believe that the problem of civil and industrial defence is still soluble, and that the solution is known at least in broad outline. This goes far beyond the scope of the Ministry of Defence or of the Home Office: any answer must be the joint answer of something like a score of home departments.[1]

Finally, there is the problem of industrial mobilisation. This is the concern apparently of the production departments of the Admiralty and Ministry of Supply: but the problem, like that of civil defence, is far wider. It can be resolved only by a continuous weighing of priorities often in small and highly technical matters. What sacrifice in quantity or efficiency of production should be made now as an insurance for the maintenance and expansion of output in time of war? This is fundamentally the old question of what share of national resources should be expended on defence, the issue which made the Victorian Chancellor of the Exchequer the second man in the Cabinet, and is not one which can be resolved or even eased by departmental reorganisation.

5. EXTERNAL AFFAIRS

Before 1914 the Foreign Office had two formidable rivals, the Colonial Office and the Government of India, and British foreign policy was largely a resultant of these three competing forces: even Lord Salisbury was forced to manipulate rather than to direct his colleagues. To all appearances, the Foreign Office is now stronger than ever before. *The Colonial Office* is still important in many spheres, Palestine (until 1948) for instance and Malaya, but it is no longer the explosive force that it was in the time of Joseph Chamberlain. Its offshoot, *the Commonwealth Relations Office*, is a department professionally modest in its claims and gentle in its manners, and what was once *the India Office* has now to all appearances been absorbed into its tradition. Internally, the Foreign Office has attained at last its goal of independence and equality *vis-à-vis* the Home Civil

[1]This issue was most interestingly debated on the Committee and Report stages of the Civil Defence Act, 1949. *Hansard*, 30th November and 3rd December, 1948.

Service: and it has paid only a small price in measures of "democratisation" which ought in the end to strengthen its hand by extending its field of recruitment and raising the quality of its staff. In addition, it has brought under effective control these two considerable empires, the Control Office for Germany and Austria, and the British Council.

Nevertheless, there are two difficulties in sight. *In the first place*, the war made it clear (and the peace has made it even clearer) that open propaganda and secret subversion are in the twentieth century weapons of national policy which we will neglect at our peril. We like to think that no good comes of them in the long run;[1] but unfortunately the short run is now strategically vital to us, and we can no longer refuse to believe that these weapons are in the short run very effective. This was an unhappy corner of our war organisation[2] because at the outset it was regarded with some distaste, and its importance was not clearly felt until the fall of France. In the end a single task was divided between three agencies: *the Ministry of Information*, responsible for propaganda in the Far East and in neutral and unoccupied allied countries: the *Political Warfare Executive* (P.W.E.) (jointly controlled by the Foreign Office and the M.O.I.), responsible for propaganda intended to weaken the enemy in Europe: *the Special Operations Executive* (S.O.E.) (under the Minister of Economic Warfare), responsible for practical aid and encouragement to resistance movements in all occupied territories. In theory, each of these organisations (which were very large and complex organisations) received its political directives from the Foreign Office, its military directives from the Chiefs of Staff Committee or the Supreme Allied Commander concerned. Unfortunately there is in war no clear line between the spheres of political and military action: and (what is more) general directives often bear little relation to the details of reality in either sphere. This latter trouble particularly affected S.O.E., whose agents in occupied

[1]The Duke of Wellington (as so often) expresses the classic English view: "I always had a horror of revolutionising any country for a political object. I always said, if they rise of themselves, well and good, but do not stir them up: it is a fearful responsibility." Stanhope's "Conversations " (*World's Classics*), p. 69.
[2]It is cold comfort that the organisation in the U.S.A. was even worse.

territory (in Greece for instance and Yugoslavia) rarely had adequate communications with their base, and were forced continually to extemporise policy for themselves as best they could. In such circumstances a man is guided much more by his own judgment and by the spirit of the organisation in which he has been trained than by directives which are usually obsolete before they reach him.

This confusion of responsibilities arose in part from an instinctive feeling among politicians that these new powers were too great and too sinister to trust to any single Minister in a democracy: there was perhaps also some suggestion that propaganda and subversion were not fit work for gentlemen of the Foreign Office. But effective reorganisation was deferred mainly by overwork and diffidence in the Foreign Office, which was overburdened with other business and had neither men nor time to spare for the direction of this new "Fourth Arm." It seems pretty clear from past experience that the only hope of combining discretion with energy in this field lies in strong direct control by the Foreign Office: but if this is to be successful it will mean that a good many diplomats must revert to a conception of diplomacy more primitive than that of the nineteenth century, which still lingers in the corners of Sir Gilbert Scott's quadrangle.

In the second place, it cannot escape any reader of the newspapers that a great part of our foreign affairs is at present conducted by agencies other than the Foreign Office. This is not only a matter of the defence departments, whose role has been exceptionally important ever since the staff talks with France in 1906. International agreements are regularly negotiated by the Treasury, Board of Trade, Ministry of Food, Ministry of Transport, Ministry of Labour, Ministry of Civil Aviation, and other economic departments, and there must be eminent members of the Home Civil Service who have initialled more diplomatic documents than any diplomat. In detail, these agreements are technical and uninspiring: in sum, they make up our economic foreign policy, which involves inescapable commitments of other kinds. The Foreign Office are certainly not masters of the foreign policy which thus emerges: are they even alert enough to know what it is? It is now obvious that foreign policy cannot be made in a single office: it is all the more important that there should be a single office competent to tell the Cabinet clearly and promptly what is implied in the dispersed activities of the technical departments.

The simple picture of "external affairs" has, therefore, changed profoundly since it was reviewed by the Haldane Committee in 1918. On the one hand, every internal department has a share in foreign policy: on the other hand, the foreign policy of a great power now implies the existence of executive agencies of political warfare which cannot be neglected even in what is formally a time of peace. It is not clear that the great Foreign Office reforms[1] put forward by Mr. Eden in 1943 are well adapted to these new conditions. In effect, these reforms proceed on the old assumption that the conduct of diplomacy is a proper subject for a specialised profession. They extend the range of that profession, they throw it more widely open to talent, they provide better facilities for training: but they do not contemplate the possibility that the profession itself may be obsolescent. In theory there is much to be said now for scrapping the old profession and rebuilding on a different model. On the one hand (it is said) professional diplomats are notoriously ignorant of the foreign countries in which they work, and often have difficulty in believing that there are real people in them outside official circles. Therefore, let us develop the Foreign Office Research Department until it becomes a comprehensive and influential intelligence service, whose specialists will know what is "really" happening, and see that the truth is heard in Whitehall. On the other hand, the Foreign Office may easily miss the implications in foreign policy of the economic and social activities of the collectivist state. Therefore, let us abolish the Foreign Service, and insist on a free interchange of talent and experience between all the departments of state. This unfortunately is a pretty picture, not a practicable plan: we must, for better or for worse, make do with what we have got, the living mechanism of the Foreign Office. The Foreign Office is in some ways a spinsterish and rather rigid

[1]See Cmd.6420 of 1943: and *International Affairs*, Vol. XXII, p. 57, article by Mr. Ashton-Gwatkin.

creature, but it is full of intelligence, and not in the least blind to the need for self-improvement. The trouble is that a diplomat cannot effectively learn the scope or limitations of his own profession unless he is given some leisure when he is young: leisure in which to escape the exigencies of office routine and to study seriously either some other country or his own. The prospects of leisure are not great at present, when the Office and the Legations are understaffed and overdriven: but the Foreign Office will in due course involve itself and the rest of us in trouble if it wastes its capital by exploiting its recruits too far.

6. RESEARCH[1]

When the D.S.I.R. was set up in December 1916, a million pounds to be spread over a term of years was regarded as a generous encouragement to industrial research; probably the whole expenditure of the nation on research of every kind did not then exceed that sum each year. In 1938, the Association of Scientific Workers estimated the total cost of research at £4,000,000. By 1948, this figure had increased to £100,000,000, an appreciable fraction of a national income of about £8,750,000,000: of this £60,000,000 was spent in defence research, £30,000,000 in industry and £10,000,000 on other civil purposes (including £3,000,000 within the Ministries).[2] There is probably no other field in which there has been so great a proportionate increase in Government activity, and the increase has been warmly supported by public opinion of all political colours. What effect has this revolution had on the distribution of duties between departments? The answer is, in short, "None."

[1] Apart from the annual reports of the D.S.I.R. and the various research councils, the most useful papers here are:—*The Scientific Worker*, Vol. X, No. 4 (Nov. 1938), "The Finance of Research"; *Planning*, No. 135 of 29th November 1948: Cmd.6514 of 1944, "Scientific Research and Development": Cmd.6679 of Sept. 1945, "The Scientific Civil Service": Cmd.6824 of 1946, "Scientific Manpower": H.C.132 of 1946/47, "Third Report of Estimates Committee": Cmd.6868 of 1946, "The 'Clapham Committee' Report on Social and Economic Research: Cmd.7465 of May 1948, "1st Annual Report of the Advisory Council on Scientific Policy."

[2] Figures given by Professor Bernal, President of the Association of Scientific Workers in a B.B.C. talk on 1st September 1948 (*The Listener*, 16th September, 1948). The Select Committee identified some £76,000,000 of Government expenditure on scientific research in the Estimates for 1947/48.

The Haldane Committee were strongly in favour of the creation of a central Department of Research, but they also set out very fairly the arguments for the retention by individual departments of much control over the work to be done in their own fields; and these arguments have on the whole had the upper hand. The D.S.I.R. has developed its old activities, and has added new ones, but it has not become in any sense a central department. The administrative arguments for such a department are more obvious than ever, now that private industry and the Ministries are awake to the importance of research and are competing fiercely for limited manpower and resources: but this has been recognised not by the development of the D.S.I.R., but by the creation of two new organisations, the Advisory Council on Scientific Policy and the Defence Research Policy Committee, which share a full-time chairman and a small secretariat. The former looks to the Lord President of the Council for ministerial guidance, the latter to the Minister of Defence.

There are obvious reasons for this timidity. The Departments now see pretty clearly that control of research means control of policy, and they will fight hard to remain masters in their own houses. Nor are the researchers themselves much in love with centralisation;[1] like other interests, they are anxious for public assistance, but not for public control. It is perfectly true that public generosity to scientists can itself become a danger to scientific freedom, above all to the freedom of publication, and the position is a little eased if the researcher's liberty is not held at the discretion of a single paymaster. This is an awkward problem, socially and administratively: how are we to secure sufficient order for the rational allocation of limited resources, sufficient anarchy for the individual initiative indispensable to research? This is hard enough in the natural sciences, which seem at first sight to have nothing to do with politics: it is still worse for the social sciences which are expected to elucidate subjects on which there is confused and excitable debate among

[1]Professor Bernal and Professor Polanyi (*The Listener*, 16th September, 1948) disagree on practically everything else: but they are both certain that science should not be organised by civil servants.

74

political parties and the general public. An increase in public endowment may mean only that a higher proportion of the competent workers will be absorbed into government service, and there be muzzled by political caution and by the Official Secrets Acts.

7. PRODUCTION AND SUPPLIES

These two Haldane categories must be taken together, since we have departed very far from the scheme of things indicated by the Committee. As they saw it, in the light of their experience before 1914, there was here a tripartite division. *First*, there was a great department, the Board of Trade, concerned with the regulation and encouragement of private enterprise in industry and commerce: and a lesser department, the Board of Agriculture and Fisheries, charged with similar responsibilities as regards food production. *Second*, there was scarcely one government department which did not purchase supplies for its own needs in the open market on some scale, large or small: there was limited centralisation of supplies only in the hands of the Office of Works and the Stationery Office. *Third*, there was one great nationalised industry, the Post Office, which was conducted with tolerable efficiency by a staff of civil servants supervised by a Minister of the Crown: a little tendentiously, the Committee puts forward the Service departments as further examples of this technique of nationalisation.

From this they deduced, without committing themselves to details, three principles of importance. *First*, it was obvious (at least to the key members of the Committee) that further industries would in due course be nationalised. In 1918 it seemed plain that the way to combine efficiency with democratic control was that each industry or group of industries should be run directly, by a Ministry represented on the front bench in the House of Commons. *Second*, there would be obvious difficulties if one Ministry were to be made responsible both for a nationalised industry and for the regulation of private industry competing in the same field. *Third*, it would make for economy that all government purchases in the open market should be handled by a single organisation.

These are admirable principles which still make good sense, but the current of events has been too much for them. The list which has been given enumerates fifteen major economic departments, including the Scottish Office, and not one of them is intelligible except as a matter of political history—in part the history of party politics, in part that of pressure groups inside and outside Whitehall. Most of them have been formed by budding off activities from the older departments, in particular from the Board of Trade, from which came the Ministries of Supply (in part), Food, Transport, Fuel and Power, Labour: the Ministry of Supply descends also in part from the War Office and the Air Ministry, the Ministry of Civil Aviation from the Air Ministry. The Colonial Office and the Scottish Office have been pushed into the economic field by political forces which they have on the whole resisted while they could. The Ministry of Works, finally, is a curious case in which the logic of centralised purchasing has led in due course to the assumption of responsibility for a single industry—the building industry: a responsibility confused by the existence of another department, the Ministry of Health, whose housing programme is politically the master of the industry in question. In addition to all these, there is a long list of semi-independent public corporations, each of which bears some ill-defined share of responsibility for national policy in the field of production.

This is a jungle in which the theoretical student is at a loss for clues. Its inhabitants are, he knows, competent and well-intentioned persons; it is to be hoped that they are familiar with the jungle paths which link their little plots of cultivation, and that they live on reasonably good terms with their neighbours. But if they do not, there is nothing anyone outside can do to help them, because no one outside the jungle can hope to understand it. When the inhabitants have leisure, their clearings may extend and their paths become recognisable as highways: but for the moment they are doing pretty well if they can keep the jungle at bay. The autocracy of economic planners is not a danger one can take seriously at the moment.

76

8. JUSTICE AND HEALTH

It is convenient also to link Justice and Health. They may seem more oddly matched than Production and Supplies, but the plans of Lord Haldane and Sir Robert Morant here ran together and the same cause has defeated both.

A true Ministry of Health was to be formed by the transfer to the Home Office of the Local Government Board's responsibility for the machinery of local government; and the Home Office was to acquire also the Lord Chancellor's responsibility for the machinery of justice (though not for appointments) and to give impetus to the necessary reforms in private law and in the organisation of the courts.

It is relevant to notice here that there is one rather startling omission in the Committee's analysis of the functions of Government; there is no reference at all to the maintenance of public order, which theorists of diverse schools are pretty well agreed in treating as the first function of Government. One peculiarity of the English constitution is that this responsibility has always been widely diffused, except in rare periods of stress, and this diffusion still persists. Responsibility for police is divided between the Home Office, the Scottish Office and over 150 local authorities, to say nothing of the Government of Northern Ireland. Responsibility for the supervision of local authorities is divided between many departments, and the most important of these is emphatically not the Home Office, but the Ministry of Health. Responsibility for the trial of offenders and for the framework or public and private law is almost lost to sight between the Lord Chancellor, the Home Office, the Lord Chief Justice, and the lesser law officers of the Crown.

This system is the creation of time and chance, but its retention is not so fortuitous as it seems. It is plain in theory that centralisation here means centralisation of power in its most naked sense: and theory in this instance has teeth in it, for two of the strongest vested interests in England, the local authorities and the legal profession, would fight to the end against the creation of an efficient and powerful Ministry of the Interior. It is almost universally recognised that our system of justice and our system of local government are urgently in need of reform; that it is ludicrous to have a Ministry of Health which is also a Ministry of Housing and half a Ministry of the Interior: that the duties of the Home Office are only a little less absurd than those of the Lord Chancellor. But it is just as clear that the ice is here particularly thin: politicians by instinct give it a wide berth, and the general public, still more the special publics concerned, are extremely averse to change. The first essential for reform is public and professional interest and understanding: until these are stirred it is useless to think that anything substantial can be achieved by reorganisation in Whitehall.

9. Conclusion

In so hasty a survey attention concentrates on the anomalies, and the impression given has perhaps been one of general confusion and inefficiency. If so, it is essential to correct it. We can comfort ourselves greatly by a glance at our neighbours. Washington is a joke of quite a different order of magnitude from Whitehall, and when it ceases to amuse it terrifies. There is immense energy and ability in American administration: there is also a total lack of continuity, and the co-ordination of policy is at the mercy of the trivial accidents of politics. Islands of stability are beginning to emerge, but they are still exceptional, and (apart from the Service departments) they are not important on the higher levels of policy. Departmental tradition still has very little weight in American Government, and the lack of it is quite as dangerous as its presence in excess. In France the traditions of the public offices have been very strong, but they are apparently in decline. Administrative skill still exists, or the national recovery since 1944 would have been impossible: but corruption, which has always been endemic, spread more widely during the occupation and it has not yet receded. Further, in the prevailing instability, every political party has become increasingly eager to pack the key departments with its own supporters. In spite of all efforts at reform, there is an uneasy feeling in the air that the structure of French bureaucracy, which has held up the French State through so many troubles, is beginning to crack at last. In Germany subordinates in the professional services appear to have remained competent and fairly honest to the end: but by that time the incomparable machine had been largely wrecked by monkey-house politics in Berlin, and by corruption widely disseminated through the hierarchy of the Nazi Party. Germany this time waged war less efficiently than Britain. Russia we can judge only by a few hints and by what we know of Tsarist bureaucracy: but there is no reason to believe that like causes do not still produce like effects. The few glimpses we are allowed suggest that there is much the same old amalgam of *paperasserie* and irresponsible individual energy and irresponsible terroristic discipline.

No doubt there are some smaller countries in which the administration is simpler and more responsive than ours. But in public administration differences of scale readily become differences of kind, and comparisons with (for instance) Switzerland, Norway or New Zealand are plainly unfair. The administration of a Great Power is a very different problem: the difficulties are enormous, as are the responsibilities. It is not too much to boast that with all its imperfections the British administration is more intelligent, more supple, more coherent than that of any other Great Power: and that it has shown astonishing vitality and efficiency during a period of intense strain and rapid change. This great work has been done largely in defiance of the only theoretical principle we possess, that of the Haldane Committee. Can anything fresh be learned from the experience of thirty years?

In the *first* place, it is clear that the Committee's classification of departments is in some ways clumsy, in others incomplete. It is simpler to work (as the Cabinet now appears to do) with five main groups: the three classic functions of government, law and order, external affairs, and defence: the sphere of finance as "ways and means," which has now expanded to include responsibility for all national production and trade: the rather miscellaneous sphere of social services, which is on the whole the sphere of consumption or "supply," the things which we really want as individuals. There are, of course, aspects of the social services, such as nutrition, health and education, which contribute in their turn to "national efficiency" for production

or defence: these dividing lines are nowhere very firm, and must
be treated as matters of relative convenience, not of principle.

In the *second* place, certain important functions have
emerged which cannot be evaded much longer, though our
organisation for handling them is still primitive. First, there is
the continuous review of national resources and their allocation
between the great spheres of national activity. We are not
prepared now (if we ever were) to submit ourselves wholly to
allocation by free competition and the price mechanism, yet
we have not evolved a substitute. These priorities are primarily
a field of political decision, which cannot be shuffled off on any
sort of "Civil General Staff"; but even political decisions require
a foundation of independent expert knowledge which is at
present provided only in a rudimentary way by the Cabinet
Office, the Treasury, the Board of Trade, and the Ministry
of Town and Country Planning. Second, there is the process
of public information. The range of government is now so
vast that the old constitutional channel of formal statements
by responsible ministers is altogether too narrow for the
information which the public must have. We demand to know
more of what the departments are doing; and, at the same
time, we grumble when they defend themselves, because in so
doing they spend public money to justify the administration of
the political party in power. A return made to Parliament in
February 1947 indicated that this task was then discharged by
some 330 civil servants above the clerical level, divided between
the Public Relations sections of the departments and the
Central Office of Information under the Lord President:[1] a
substantial force which is not likely to be much reduced by any
Government. Third, there is the continuous scrutiny and supervision of the whole immense administrative organisation,
which employs directly a quarter of the working population of
the country and regulates the working lives of all the rest.
Fortunately, Parliament has begun to interest itself both in the
Organisation and Methods work of the Treasury, and in what

[1]*Hansard*, 3rd February, 1947, "Written Answers," col. 296. See also *Planning*,
No. 230 of 2nd February, 1945, and the first annual report of the Central Office of
Information (Cmd.7567). A committee of enquiry into the size of these staffs was
appointed by the Government in October, 1948.

is vaguely called an "efficiency audit" of the nationalised industries. It is clear, too, from Sir Edward Bridges' evidence before the Estimates Committee, that he is anxious to root out the tradition that higher civil servants are primarily the Minister's secretaries and are only remotely responsible for the morale and efficiency of their subordinates: but, as he says, "you do not change the whole outlook of a profession over-night." Meantime, all first-rate administrators are extremely busy with the trees, and it is no one's business to observe the configuration of the wood. This function of self-consciousness is discharged, if at all, only by the small central staff of Organ-isation and Methods and by a handful of academic students in the Universities.

It will be noticed that each of these functions is of great political importance. They require organisation, but the impulse to create it must come largely from the Cabinet and from the House of Commons, not from the professional administrators.

Third, the allocation of functions by services to be rendered rather than by clients to be served is a good principle as a principle of cheap administration. It is the most economical way in which to use a limited staff of experts. But it is not necessarily economical for the public; there are other important and productive persons besides those in government service, and it may sometimes be more wasteful to send the public on circuit through a series of different offices than to create single offices capable of handling all the business brought to them by a particular class of clients. It is now one of the functions of government to save the time and temper of housewives and business men, and in this cause it may often be necessary to break the Haldane principle even at the expense of some slight rise in departmental estimates and in the quarterly returns of the Civil Service establishment. The old principle can be of over-riding importance only when the number of experts available is very limited and it is clearly slow and wasteful to train more.

Fourth, it is clear now that the principle is one of a relatively low grade. It is of great importance to the distribution of work

F

between specialised branches and divisions, but it has little relevance to the higher organisation of the great departments of state. It is now quite impossible that the leaders of any great department should be specialists in any aspect of their day's work, whatever they may be by origin and training. If any issue reaches the "policy level", its implications ramify throughout Whitehall: the man to settle it is not the specialist in one implication, but the man who sees all the implications quickly, asks for advice in the right quarters quickly, and understands the advice given him. The administrative class has served us well in the past, and its tradition is now more important than ever before: it must be trained hard and used unsparingly to break down the departmentalism of the expert. This does not mean that admission to the class should be limited to those with a general education and a capacity for literary examinations: on the contrary, it will be all the better for an influx of men with specialist training, either direct from the Universities or later, provided that they can then pass beyond their own specialism.

Fifth, we are more sceptical now than were, for instance, the Webbs in the 1890's regarding the advantages of an administrative "Samurai" who will by pure reason introduce economy, efficiency, sweetness and light into the processes of government. The Haldane Committee was composed of persons exceptional in ability, in experience and in good will, but we can see after thirty years that their conclusions were largely wrong, or at least irrelevant. The great changes in administration have come about through causes partly fortuitous, partly political, but on the whole outside the range of administrative planning. The political forces are sometimes positive in their effects on administration: as, for instance, in the long-term trend which is raising the status of the Scottish Office or in the brief accidents which made the creation of a Ministry of Supply in 1939 symbolic of a resolute foreign policy, or the creation of M.A.P. in 1940 symbolic of resistance to the end. More often they are negative, there is a sort of dumb political deadweight which blocks certain forms of centralisation. In this, sound democratic instincts often mingle with vested interest: it would almost certainly be wrong in a democracy to concentrate further the responsibility for law and order,[1] or for higher education, or for scientific and social research, or for public information. On the other hand we might gain much and lose nothing by more effective central control of foreign policy or of production: but even here there are instincts which rebel, and they are worth listening to, even when they are illogical.

Finally, it is now certain, for better or for worse, that the Haldane Committee were correct in their tacit assumption that the departments exist in their own right as elements in the constitution. It is impossible now to return to the age which regarded them as extensions of the Minister's private office. A good Minister can control his department, he can even change it, but the department will outlive him none the less. It is a pity, however, that the Committee did not recognise at all clearly that departments are staffed by human beings, and that a department or a division has as real and individual an existence as any other human community. In planning a reorganisation it is fatal to forget that what you are handling is a group or groups of men and women at work. A branch or a department may be a theoretical monstrosity and yet be a "happy ship"; and traditionally a "happy ship" is the only efficient ship.

By the compulsion of events almost every department has since 1939 expanded and contracted and suffered countless changes of pattern. It is not as common as it should be to find in them teams which have worked long together, which work smoothly and which enjoy their work: and when they exist it is a crime to break them in pieces in the name of efficiency or economy. Such a change will secure neither of these things, though it may put a better face in the statistics. Much reorganisation is inevitable; but beyond that large minimum the presumption should be that dislocation will do more harm than good. "We do it wrong, being so majestical, to offer it the show

---

[1] *cf*. Sir Harold Scott, Commissioner of Metropolitan Police, in a lecture at Cambridge (*The Times*, 4th March, 1949), "We who have experience of the work of the O.G.P.U. and the Gestapo can understand better than our fathers the fears that attended the birth of the Metropolitan Police, and our experience has reinforced the conviction that, whatever else is apt for nationalisation, the police are not."

of violence" might be addressed even to such an enormity as the Ministry of Supply; it is certainly apt for the Lord Chancellor or the Treasury or the Home Office. What the departments most need now is time to get their breath and look around them: at another season may come complacency and absence of mind, and it will be time then to talk of first principles and radical reform.

CHAPTER IV

ADMINISTRATIVE LAW
IN ENGLAND, 1919-1948

by Professor William A. Robson

1. Changing Conceptions of the Subject

If one is to discuss the development of a branch of knowledge or an aspect of government during a particular period, it is essential that the subject-matter of the study should be clearly defined. The scope of a branch of knowledge may grow larger or smaller without necessarily affecting the nature of the subject-matter; but if the subject-matter itself change, any treatment of it which fails to take account of the change through time is likely to be seriously out of focus. As the prevailing views concerning the nature of administrative law have undergone substantial changes during the past 30 years I shall begin by showing the character of these changes.

In 1919 and throughout the following decade the view prevailed that there was no such thing as administrative law in England. Dicey's treatise on the *Law of the Constitution*, first published in 1885, dominated the minds of educated Englishmen for the next 30 or 40 years, and it was due to his teaching that a complete misunderstanding of both French and English administrative law existed. Dicey ignored or overlooked most of the great body of French *droit administratif*. He merely drew attention to certain features of it which he quite wrongly considered gave the State exceptional and extensive privileges. He noticed, first, that in France the rights of the State are determined by special rules not applicable to private individuals; second, that the courts of law are without jurisdiction in matters concerning the State and suits against the government are tried by administrative courts; third, that special protection is afforded to officials in respect of wrongful acts committed in the course of their official duties.[1]

Dicey was right in asserting that there is no counterpart in

[1] *Law of the Constitution*, 9th edition, chapter 12.

England of the administrative jurisdiction of the *Conseil d'État* and the prefectoral courts in France. He was utterly wrong in contending that the French system is antithetic to the rule of law and is the embodiment of arbitrary or irresponsible power. Unfortunately, however, students of law and government readily accepted the inference that because there is no *droit administratif* in England we are therefore without a system of administrative law. This, too, was entirely wrong. Dicey's last-hour recantation of his earlier opinions in a short article[1] did little to modify the widespread influence of the mistaken views which he had propagated so effectively. I recall Professor Berthélemy, of the University of Paris, saying in a lecture delivered in London many years ago that Dicey had once remarked to him "In England we know nothing of administrative law and we wish to know nothing about it."

By 1930 a change of outlook had begun to appear. Sir Cecil Carr's masterly little book, *Delegated Legislation*, published in 1921, had drawn attention to the importance of the legislative powers exercised by Ministers and other executive bodies. My own work, *Justice and Administrative Law*, first published in 1928, gave a detailed account of the judicial functions exercised by a great variety of administrative tribunals. In 1929 Lord Hewart issued his polemical tirade against the civil service in *The New Despotism* and the late F. J. Port published a treatise entitled *Administrative Law* which dealt mainly with the legislative and judicial powers conferred on administrative organs. Dr. C. K. Allen followed suit in 1931 with *Bureaucracy Triumphant*.

This literature had its effect in undermining the belief that England is a country which has no administrative law. The complacent contrast between happy Englishmen free from *droit administratif* and unhappy Frenchmen subject to its terrors faded quietly out of the picture. A new misconception took its place. This was the notion that administrative law in Britain consists wholly or mainly of delegated legislation on the one hand and administrative justice on the other. This idea was encouraged—implicitly rather than explicitly—by the appoint-

[1] "The Development of Administrative Law in England," *Law Quarterly Review*, Vol. 31, p. 148.

ment of the Committee on Ministers' Powers in 1929 to deal with these two hotly-debated questions. The only explicit reference to so narrow a conception was the language used by the Committee in rejecting my proposals. Under the heading "Inexpediency of establishing a system of administrative law" the Report referred to "A regularised system of administrative Courts and administrative Law, such as Mr. Robson proposes. . . ."[1] The Committee here identified an administrative court with "a system of administrative law"—a clear reversion to Dicey's view of *droit administratif*.

We have not yet wholly emerged from the belief that administrative law can be defined in terms of the legislative and judicial powers of executive organs. There are, however, signs that a more comprehensive view of the subject is gaining ground. Teachers of public law in the Universities and in the professional Law Schools are reaching out towards a wider conception.[2] Modern legal literature, too, reveals an expanding view of the subject-matter of administrative law.[3]

There is still much ground to be covered before administrative law is recognised to be no more and no less than the law relating to public administration; but acceptance of that definition, which is the only logical one, is now only a matter of time. It is in this sense that I shall use the term here.

Before leaving this question of how the subject is understood in its application to Britain, a further word must be said about the attitude of Englishmen towards French *droit administratif*. Very few people on this side of the Channel now hold Dicey's views of *droit administratif*. Even lawyers of conservative outlook are prepared to admit that the French system offers superior guarantees of justice and better facilities for redress to the

[1] Report, Cmd. 4060/1932, p. 110.
[2] See, for example, the syllabus for Administrative Law in the regulations for the LL.B. and LL.M. degrees in the University of London; also the syllabus of Public Law in the LL.B. examination at Cambridge, which contains 3 papers (out of a total of 4) dealing exclusively with Administrative Law.
[3] *Cf.* E. C. S. Wade and G. Godfrey Phillips: *Constitutional Law*, 3rd ed., Part VII, "Administrative Law"; Stephen's *Commentaries on the Laws of England*, 20th ed., Vol. I, Book II, "Constitutional and Administrative Law"; Sir Cecil Carr, K.C.: *Concerning English Administrative Law* (1941). Sir Alfred Denning: *Freedom Under the Law*; Robert S. W. Pollard (Ed.) *Administrative Tribunals at Work*; G. W. Keeton: *The Elementary Principles of Jurisprudence* (2nd. Edition) Ch. XX.

citizen in his dealings with the State than the English courts provide.[1] At an Anglo-French legal conference organised by the Law Society in London in 1947 there was no disposition on the part of the English lawyers to assume that these matters are better ordered in Britain.

Yet in 1942 an astonishing incident occurred during a Secret Session of Parliament. Mr. Winston Churchill was explaining to the House of Commons the reasons which had led the Allied forces which had invaded French North Africa to accept the services of Admiral Darlan, who was closely associated with the Vichy regime, and generally believed to be hostile to the Allied cause. Mr. Churchill told the House of Commons on that occasion that in France, which had experienced so many convulsions since the revolution of 1789, there had grown up a principle founded on the '*droit administratif*' which governs the action of many French officers and officials in times of stress and upheaval. This highly legalistic attitude leads them to enquire whether there is a direct, unbroken chain of lawful command linking those who wield power with those who previously possessed lawful authority. They regard this as more important than moral, national or international considerations. It was in accordance with orders and authority transmitted or declared to be transmitted by Marshal Petain that the French troops in North Africa had taken sides with the Allied troops against the German and Italian forces there. This, Mr. Churchill contended, was the justification for using Darlan.

This confusion in the mind of the Prime Minister between *légalité* and *droit administratif* is a remarkable example of Dicey's influence on the mind of the great war leader.[2]

2. The Growth of Administrative Law

I have suggested that administrative law should be regarded as the law relating to public administration, in the same way as commercial law consists of the law relating to commerce, or land law the law relating to land. There is, however, an important distinction between administrative law and most other

[1]See C. K. Allen: *Law and Orders*, pp. 164, 171.
[2]*Winston Churchill, Secret Session Speeches*, compiled by Charles Eade, pub. 1946, pp. 81-82.

branches of law. The sources of administrative law include not only the law controlling public administration (i.e. Statutes, common law and equity), but also the law emanating from the executive organs in the exercise of their duly authorised powers. Thus, statutory instruments, administrative orders and the determinations of administrative tribunals can be as authentic sources of administrative law as legislation and decisions of the Courts. Moreover, just as the usages and conventions of the Constitution form an important part of constitutional law, so the usages and conventions of the Executive form an essential part of administrative law.

The corpus of English administrative law has grown enormously during the past 30 years. It is now so large that one mind could not possibly master all its multitudinous branches in any detail. One has only to glance at the great legal treatises devoted to public health or housing to realise the overwhelming magnitude and complexity of these specialised ramifications.

The phenomenal growth of administrative law has mainly been caused by the expansion of public administration in almost every direction. The rise of town and country planning, for example, has led to a substantial body of law on that subject. The same is true of most of the other functions of government which have developed during the period. The administrative law relating to national insurance, housing, fire brigades, conditions of labour and industrial relations, public utilities, health services, transport regulation, and many other public services is far greater to-day than it was in 1919. Most of this law originates in Statute and statutory instrument. The primacy of legislation in this field can be seen by glancing at recent volumes of the Statutes of the realm or statutory instruments. The great majority of Acts of Parliament passed and Ministerial regulations made in recent years relate to matters of public administration.

3. ORGANISATION OF THE EXECUTIVE

(a) *Central Departments*

One of the most important but least studied branches of administrative law is that which relates to the organisation, constitution, procedures and general functioning of public authorities. What changes have occurred here during the past 30 years?

Prior to the war of 1914-18 only a very few departments of the central government had a statutory basis. In this respect the Local Government Board, the Board of Education and the Board of Agriculture and Fisheries stood almost alone. The High Officers of State, such as the Lord Chancellor, the Chancellor of the Exchequer, the several Secretaries of State, the Lord Privy Seal, the Lord President of the Council, the First Lord of the Admiralty, and so on, were in law "emanations of the Crown". They and their departments were expressions of the royal prerogative; and although most of them had come to exercise statutory as well as prerogative powers, the legal authority for their existence derived from the constitutional usage of an earlier age when all executive power resided in the King.

During the war of 1914-18 several departments were established by Act of Parliament, including the Ministries of Labour and Pensions in 1916. Since then all new departments have been constituted by statute with the exception of those set up between 1939 and 1945 for war purposes. The latter were initiated by Order in Council under the Provisions of the Ministers of the Crown (Emergency Appointments) Act 1939.

In consequence we can discover from the statute book and the volumes of Statutory Rules and Orders quite a lot about the modern departments but scarcely anything about the older ones. There are Acts of Parliament authorising His Majesty to appoint a Minister of Health, a Minister of Transport, a Minister of Agriculture and Fisheries, a Minister of Town and Country Planning, a Minister of Civil Aviation, a Minister of National Insurance, and so on. The general scope of their respective duties is laid down in a 'fanfare' section in each Act. Thus, the Ministry of Health Act, 1919, provides that

"It shall be the duty of the Minister, in the exercise and performance of any powers and duties transferred to or conferred upon him by or in pursuance of this Act, to take all such steps as may be desirable to secure the preparation, effective carrying out and co-ordination of measures conducive to the health of the people, including measures for the prevention and cure of diseases, the avoidance of fraud in connection with alleged remedies therefor, the treatment of physical and mental defects, the treatment and care of the blind, the initiation and direction of research, the collection, preparation, publication, and dissemination of information and statistics relating thereto, and the training of persons for health services."

There is much to be said in favour of giving each Government department a statutory basis. It makes for coherence in the scheme of central organisation. It enables Ministers, Parliament, the Public Accounts Committee, the Treasury and the public to know what is expected of each department—and especially of new ones. It may prevent inter-departmental conflicts and friction by revealing in advance possible causes of overlapping or duplication.

The importance of these 'fanfare' sections is, however, political, administrative and financial rather than legal. Moreover, the inclusion in a 'machinery' Act of a section indicating the general scope of a Minister's duties does not imply that any action which he may take outside the terms of the section is necessarily *ultra vires*. The doctrine of *ultra vires* may apply to a Minister who exceeds his statutory powers or acts without powers in such a way as to injure a citizen in respect of his property or person. It does not apply where no such injury is committed, even if the particular act is not within the scope of the Minister's functions as laid down by statute. In short, these 'fanfare' sections, like many other legislative provisions in administrative law, are not susceptible of judicial review or enforcement. They lay down a pattern of administrative behaviour which is in practice followed by the executive; but the sanctions are political and financial rather than legal. Enactments of this kind, although they contain many non-justiceable provisions, are an authentic source of administrative law.

Mention has already been made of the Ministers of the Crown (Emergency Appointments) Act, 1939, which can be used to create new Ministers and departments by Order in Council "for the purpose of exercising functions connected with the prosecution of any war in which His Majesty may be engaged". This innovation was extensively used during the Second World War, when it effected a valuable saving of Parliamentary time.

Most of the powers and duties of Government departments are to-day statutory; and it is customary for Parliament to specify in each Act the particular Minister on whom it confers a power or imposes a duty. During the war it was possible to transfer powers and duties between certain departments by Orders in Council.[1] This method is now made permanently available without restrictions by the Ministers of the Crown (Transfer of Functions) Act, 1947, which also authorises the Government to close down redundant departments and to allocate their residual functions to other departments.

This measure greatly increases the flexibility of the Governmental machine. It enables the responsibilities of departments to be transferred quickly and easily in order to meet new situations or to enhance administrative efficiency. It avoids the necessity for the Government having to occupy Parliamentary time with purely administrative matters of a non-political character.

Considerable changes of this kind were made during the war. They included the transfer of the Factory Inspectorate from the Home Office to the Ministry of Labour and National Service, and the transfer of the Board of Trade's functions under the Merchant Shipping Acts to the Ministry of Transport.

(b) Local Government

There has been—unfortunately—no major change in the organisation of local government during the past 30 years, apart from the abolition of the Boards of Guardians in 1929. We still carry on with the organisational pattern laid down towards the end of the nineteenth century, though, as I shall show later,

---

[1] Under the provisions of the Ministers of the Crown (Emergency Appointments) Act, 1939, Section 5. This Act was repealed by S.R. & O. 1946 No. 563 made under the Ministers of the Crown and House of Commons Disqualification Act 1942.

there have been very large changes in the powers of local authorities.

Nevertheless, the legal basis of local government has been immensely improved. In 1920 the administrative law relating to the constitution, general powers and procedure of borough councils was contained in the Municipal Corporation Acts of 1835 and 1882; that of county councils in the Local Government Act, 1888; that of district and parish councils in the Local Government Act, 1894. The Public Health Act, 1875 had to be consulted not only on public health matters but also in order to ascertain the powers and duties of district auditors. There were very considerable variations of principle and practice of a quite irrational kind between these several statutes.

From 1930 onwards a determined effort towards simplification, consolidation and codification was made by the Ministry of Health, for which that department deserves great credit. The Minister set up a Departmental Committee to consider the consolidation of the law relating to local authorities and local government and public health. The most important result is the Local Government Act, 1933, which forms a constitutional code for local authorities of all classes outside London. The metropolis was dealt with in a similar way by the London Government Act 1939

The Local Government Act, 1933 is a legislative landmark. It is by no means merely an affair of scissors and paste. It represents a great rationalising and systematising achievement which has immensely simplified the task of everyone concerned with local government. It is perhaps the nearest approach to a code to be found on the English statute book.

Similar efforts were made by the Ministry of Health to consolidate and clean up other branches of law concerning the functions of local authorities. These led to the passing of the Public Health Act, 1936; the Housing Act, 1936; the Food and Drugs Act, 1938, and several other statutes.

The arrangements for altering areas and authorities have been radically changed in recent years. In 1920 the creation of county boroughs and the extension of their boundaries was carried out by Provisional Order made by the Minister of

93

Health under the Local Government Act, 1888. This system had resulted in the county councils suffering heavy losses of population, territory and rateable value. They were not disposed to endure their discontents lightly; and both they and the county districts forcibly expressed their dissatisfaction before the Royal Commission on Local Government (1925-9). In consequence of the recommendations contained in the first report of this Commission the Local Government (County Boroughs and Adjustments) Act, 1926 provided that in future all opposed proposals for the creation of county boroughs or the extension of their boundaries should proceed by way of private Bill; and that the minimum limit of 50,000 population hitherto required of a borough seeking county borough status should be raised to 75,000. This Act made it far more difficult in practice for county boroughs to extend their boundaries or for non-county boroughs to become county boroughs.[1]

The Local Government, Act 1929 provided for the first time for a systematic review of county district areas and authorities throughout the country. Each county council was required to submit to the Minister of Health proposals relating to county district areas and authorities within the administrative county, after consulting the councils concerned. The Minister could then accept, amend or reject these proposals. Unfortunately the areas and authorities of county councils and county boroughs were entirely excluded from this review, which thus became of secondary importance.

In 1945 the Local Government Boundary Commission was established by Act of Parliament.[2] The Commission represented an entirely new approach to the vexed problem of local government organisation. The Commission was independent of local authorities or their associations. It was subject to regulations prescribing general principles which the Minister of Health might make for the guidance of the Commission after consulting the associations of local authorities. It had also to keep

[1]For a detailed discussion of the structural problems of local government see W. A. Robson: *The Development of Local Government*, Prologue and Part I, Second (Revised) Edition, 1948. As to London, see W. A. Robson: *The Government and Misgovernment of London* (2nd Edition).
[2]Local Government (Boundary Commission) Act, 1945.

within the powers conferred upon it by Parliament. It could not, for example, replace Manchester County Borough Council by a new Manchester County Council; nor combine county and county boroughs. Despite these limitations on its powers the Local Government Boundary Commission made a hopeful start. The high calibre of its members; its independent position; its ability to form its own opinions instead of merely receiving testimony, and to put forward its own proposals instead of merely arbitrating between contested claims; the informality and cheapness of its procedure: these features marked it out as a genuine innovation with great possibilities of achieving creative reforms. As a method of effecting changes in local government organisation it was far superior to either the private Bill or the provisional order.

The Commission's reports, especially the one for 1947, stand out as the only official documents issued during the present century which attempt to deal seriously with the problems and maladies of local government. The powers of the Commission were, however, insufficient to enable it to carry out the reforms it considered desirable. The Government, instead of asking Parliament to enlarge their powers, unwisely decided to abolish the Commission.[1]

(c) *Public Service Boards, Commissions and Corporations*

Government by Commission is no new thing in England. There have been administrative organs possessing a high degree of independence of the Executive for centuries; and in the 18th and 19th centuries it was the usual practice for Parliament to set up turnpike trusts, or to appoint local bodies of commissioners to pave, light and repair the highways in particular towns, to carry out improvements, to construct and maintain the sewers. There are now perhaps 100 or 150 central authorities of one kind or another which are not under the day-to-day control of Ministers, some dating from the 18th and 19th centuries. The Charity Commission, for example, was set up in 1853.

Despite the great variety of institutions in this category which have existed for so long, it is under this heading that the most

[1] See Local Government Boundary Commission (Dissolution) Act, 1949.

spectacular developments have occurred in the period under review.

Prior to the war of 1914-18 there were only one or two public corporations which had been charged with operating public utilities. The Port of London Authority, established in 1908, was an exceptional example. But in 1919 there started to flow that stream of public bodies, beginning with the Forestry Commission and the Electricity Commission, gathering force with the Central Electricity Board, the British Broadcasting Corporation and the London Passenger Transport Board, which has finally become the swelling river which bears on its broad bosom the National Coal Board, the Bank of England, the Transport Commission, the Electricity Board, the air-line corporations, the Gas Boards, the Raw Cotton Commission, the Colonial Development Corporation, the Overseas Food Corporation, and other great undertakings.

These bodies occupy a midway territory which is bounded by law, government and economics. They are of great significance from the standpoint of administrative law. It is, however, not possible within the limits of this brief survey to do more than indicate a few of their general characteristics.

In the first place, they are with one exception the creatures of statute. The B.B.C. is an exception, since it owes its existence to a charter, supplemented by a licence and agreement granted by the Postmaster-General. The supremely important rôle which legislation plays in formulating these great administrative undertakings has not received the attention which it merits.

Secondly, powers have been conferred on these public corporations in such ample terms, that the Courts are unlikely to impose serious limitations on their activities by virtue of the doctrine of *ultra vires*.[1] Thirdly, they are liable in the Courts both in contract and in tort, subject, however, to the provisions of the Limitations Act in a modified form. Fourthly, the recent practice is to confer upon the appropriate Minister a substantial degree of potential control over the public corporation, by making him responsible for the appointment of its members and

[1]See below, p. 114-5

96

empowering him to give directions to the corporation on any matter which he considers to be in the national interest.

So far we have been concerned with organs responsible for the operation of great industrial or commercial enterprises. Mention must also be made of the numerous boards and Commissions established to conduct social services or to regulate public services. The National Assistance Board is an important example of the former, and so too are the Regional Hospital Boards and the Executive Councils set up in connection with the national medical service. The licensing authorities for goods vehicles and passenger road transport belong to the type of independent regulatory body which is to be found on a more widespread scale in the United States at the federal, state and local levels.

4. The Civil Service

We have never had a well-developed law of officers in Britain. This applies both to the civil service and the local government service. The civil service has been mainly regulated by the Prerogative, while the local government service has been dealt with largely by means of contracts made by local authorities under powers conferred by statute. In consequence, though we have for long occupied a pre-eminent position as regards the quality, integrity, devotion and political neutrality of our officials, English administrative law has little to show in this branch of public administration.

The fact that there is very little legislation or case law dealing with the civil service does not necessarily mean that there is no law and practice of the civil service. There is such a thing as customary administrative law; and I contend that there is a considerable body of customary administrative law and practice regulating the civil service. By this I mean a pattern of conduct regulating the relations between the Crown and its servants, involving obligations which are clearly formulated and regularly followed by all concerned. Such a pattern of conduct can give rise to rights and duties which are effectively recognised and observed by the administrative authorities concerned even though they are not enforceable in the courts of law. The late

G

Ernst Freund, one of the greatest American exponents of Administrative Law, wrote: "Voluntary and long continued administrative practice has many of the characteristics of law and, under favourable conditions, inherent guaranties of fairness may approach those which are generally associated with courts of justice."[1]

I do not suggest that civil servants possess formal rights against the Executive which are as valid as those arising under contracts of employment—this was shown by the recent purge of Communists and fellow-travellers; but that they do in practice have recognisable rights is incontestible.

Some progress has been made towards the formulation of the law and practice of the civil service during the past 30 years by means of Orders in Council, Treasury Regulations, Minutes and Circulars, and the compilation known as Estacode. This last-named document consists of rules or directives issued by the Treasury for the guidance of Departmental Establishment Officers. It covers a wide range of topics, ranging from salary scales to holidays. It is at present issued only to Establishment Officers, but there appears to be little reason why a body of regulations based on its provisions should not be made available for general use inside the civil service. The civil service would then, like the armed forces, have its own "King's Regulations."

Before 1927 the chief matter affecting the service which was governed by Act of Parliament was superannuation.[2] The Superannuation Act, 1870 has now been amended and extended by several subsequent statutes. Thus the Superannuation Act, 1935, provided that all pensions were in future to be calculated on the average salary for the three years preceding retirement. For the first time a civil servant was permitted to make provision for his family by surrendering a portion of his own pension in return for a grant to his wife or other dependent of equivalent actuarial value.

A feature of the Treasury pension system of increasing importance is the power to enable an established civil servant to

[1]"Administrative Law" in *Encyclopaedia of the Social Sciences*, Vol. I, p. 454.
[2]Other statutes affecting the civil service were the Sale of Offices Act, 1809, the Official Secrets Acts, 1911 and 1920, and the Public Bodies Corrupt Practices Act, 1889.

transfer to another form of "approved employment" without forfeiture of superannuation rights. It frequently happens that a civil servant is offered employment outside the Government service in some semi-official or non-official organisation. If, on the recommendation of the head of his Department, the Treasury are satisfied that it would be in the public interest for him to accept the post, they may approve such employment. The officer will then on reaching the retiring age receive the pension or gratuity which he has earned. Until recently no award could be made from public funds if the officer left the approved employment for causes other than age or ill-health. The Superannuation Act, 1946 now permits a civil servant who has taken approved employment subsequently to enter other approved employment without forfeiting his claim to superannuation.

A civil servant cannot normally receive a pension before he has completed ten years' service and reached the age of 60 unless he suffers from incapacity due to infirmity of mind or body which prevents him from doing his work properly. A further exception was introduced by the Foreign Service Act 1943, in order to facilitate the premature retirement of members of the diplomatic service who were not considered suitable for higher posts and whom it would be inexpedient to retain in the Service. The Superannuation Act 1946 enables superannuation at a higher rate to be paid to late entrants to the civil service in order to attract persons of more mature age and experience than those normally recruited by the Civil Service Commission.

In 1927, following the General Strike of 1926, Parliament took occasion to restrict the freedom of civil servants to join trade unions, other than those whose membership was confined to persons employed by the Crown. Furthermore, no civil servant could henceforth belong to a union which was affiliated to a body (such as the Trade Union Congress) which included unions containing members other than civil servants. This Act was repealed in 1947.[1]

Since 1855 there has been a steady and continuous development of Treasury control over the civil service. This control has increased substantially during the period under review. The present

[1]By the Trades Unions and Trade Disputes Act, 1947.

legal powers are derived from the Principal Order in Council made on the 22nd July, 1920 (as amended by the Order in Council of 13th September, 1947) which authorised the Treasury "to make regulations for controlling the conduct of His Majesty's Civil Establishments, and providing for the classification, remuneration, and other conditions of service of all persons employed therein, whether permanently or temporarily."

The Treasury has also to approve the regulations made by the Civil Service Commissioners prescribing the manner in which persons are to be recruited to the civil service and the conditions to be satisfied respecting the age, health, character, knowledge, nationality, and ability of candidates. Many such regulations have been made.

The primacy of the Treasury is emphasised by designating the Permanent Secretary to the Treasury as the official head of the civil service. The precise origin of this position is by no means clear. In 1926 Sir Henry Craik, M.P., himself a former civil servant, declared in the House of Commons that the Government of the day had caused a constitutional revolution by placing the Secretary of the Treasury at the summit of the civil service and "assigning to him certain functions which are arbitrarily to be attached to that newly minted office."[1] The Financial Secretary to the Treasury stated in reply that by 1872 the Permanent Secretary to the Treasury had become definitely established as head of the civil service.[2] The post is said to have been created by Treasury Minute in 1867, but the Minute disappeared for more than fifty years so that, as Sir Henry Craik remarked, "its historical value is appreciably impaired." Be that as it may, in 1920 the Government of the day formulated the principle of requiring the consent of the Prime Minister to the appointment of Permanent Heads of Departments, their deputies, Principal Financial Officers and Principal Establishment Officers. The duty was laid on the Permanent Secretary to the Treasury, on a vacancy occurring in any of these posts, of submitting advice to the Prime Minister and to the Minister in charge of the department concerned. In 1919 the Establishment Department of the Treasury was set up under the Con-

[1]194 H.C. Debates, 5S, 1926, Column 295. [2]194 H.C. Debates, 5S, 1926, Column 324.

troller of Establishments. This immensely increased the effectiveness as well as the scope of Treasury control over the civil service.

An important feature of the British civil service is its political neutrality. In 1927 the Servants of the Crown (Parliamentary Candidature) Order was issued. Under its provisions no civil servant may issue an address to electors or in any other way announce himself publicly as a candidate or prospective candidate for Parliament until he has retired or resigned from the service. An exception is made in the case of industrial employees working at the establishments maintained by the Admiralty, War Office or Air Ministry. The right to serve on a local authority is left to be dealt with by departmental regulations. The question of the political activities of civil servants has recently been considered by the Masterman Committee. The Report of this Committee is still under discussion at the time of writing.[1]

The principles of conduct which bear on the integrity of a civil servant were examined in the Ironmonger Case, 1928. The Committee of Enquiry which was set up to investigate that case formulated the standards of conduct which civil servants should observe in regard to their private financial transactions.[2] In particular, the Committee said:—

"Between the regular investment or management of a private fortune on the one hand, and speculative transactions in stocks, exchange or commodities on the other, there are obviously numerous gradations, and it may often be difficult to draw the precise line of demarcation between what is lawful and what is prohibited; it may even be inadvisable to make the attempt, because many things, though lawful, may yet be inexpedient. But some transactions fall indubitably on one side of the line rather than upon the other. It might well be desirable for a Civil Servant in all circumstances to avoid transactions wholly speculative in character; but where he is employed in any Department to which, whether rightly or wrongly, the public attribute the power of obtaining special information, such as the future course of political or financial events likely to affect the rise and fall of markets, then we assert unhesitatingly that participation in such transactions is not only undesirable or inexpedient, but wrong."

[1] Cmd.7718/1949.   [2] Cmd.5517/1927.

This report was endorsed by the Government of the day. It has frequently been referred to in Treasury circulars and the obligation to observe the standard of conduct which it lays down must now be regarded as a duty falling on all civil servants.

Certain restrictions have also been imposed on the freedom of senior civil servants to resign before reaching the normal retiring age in order to accept a business appointment. This question was dealt with in a memorandum presented by the Prime Minister to Parliament in 1937. It arose from a Report of the Royal Commission on the Private Manufacture of and Trading in Arms, 1935-36. The memorandum stated that His Majésty's Government had reached the conclusion that senior military officers and civil servants should not be permitted to take up employment in certain types of business without obtaining the prior assent of the Government. This ruling applies to officers of or above the rank of Assistant Under-Secretary of State or Principal Assistant Secretary; and certain special or technical posts to be designated by the respective departments in conjunction with the Treasury. The business appointments which fall under this ruling include those in firms holding Government contracts or receiving subsidies, loans, guarantees or other forms of financial assistance from the Government or which stand in a special relationship with the services or departments.

So far as the Courts of law are concerned, no decisions applying any new principle to civil servants have been made during the last 25 years. The absolute right of the Crown to dismiss civil servants at pleasure, regardless of any term in the contract, "however clear, however expressly provided, for employment for a specified time or that that contract can only be terminated in certain ways," was reasserted in *Rodwell v. Thomas and others*, 60 T.L.R. 431. The correctness of this doctrine was questioned in *Reilly v. Rex*[1], by Lord Atkin, who remarked that in some offices at least it is difficult to negative some contractual relations; and Denning, J., expressed the view that the judgment in Reilly's case shows that the Crown is bound by its express promises as much as any subject[2]. The Courts have

---

[1] *(1934) A.C.* at p. 179.   [2] *Robertson v. Minister of Pensions* (1948) 2 All E.R. 767.

also decided that a civil servant's expectation of a superannuation allowance is not a legal right and cannot be enforced by legal proceedings.[1]

5. LOCAL GOVERNMENT OFFICERS

The position of local government officers, in contrast to that of civil servants, is regulated largely by statute and the law of contract. There is no equivalent to the Prerogative in the sphere of local government.

The legislation regulating the local government service has been considerably extended during the period under review, but it is still far from comprehensive.

Local authorities have always had a general power to appoint such officers as the council may think necessary for the efficient discharge of their functions and to pay them such reasonable remuneration as the local authority may determine.

In addition to this general power to appoint a staff, a number of statutory provisions were scattered among numerous Acts dealing with local government which either required or permitted local authorities to appoint a Clerk or Town Clerk and certain other chief officers, such as the Medical Officer of Health, the Treasurer and Surveyor. The Local Government Act, 1933 brought all these provisions together and to some extent simplified them; but several of the enactments, such as those relating to Medical Officers, are still complex and obscure.

Under the Local Government Act, 1888 the same person was required to be both Clerk of the County Council and Clerk of the Peace for the county. The Local Government Clerk's Act, 1931 separated the two posts, giving county councils the right to appoint their own Clerks and leaving Quarter Sessions to appoint Clerks of the Peace. There are, however, complicated provisions intended to ensure that whenever possible the same man shall hold both offices.

The Local Government Act, 1933 stipulates that the remuneration of the various chief officers must be "reasonable." This statutory restriction is unnecessary, since the House of Lords

---

[1]*Nixon & Others v. Attorney-General,* 67 T.L.R., 2. 95. See also *Lucas v. Lucas and High Commissioner for India* (1932), p. 68.

decided in the Poplar wage case that even where a statute conferred power on a local authority to pay " such salaries and wages as they may think fit" there is an implied obligation to exercise the power reasonably.[1] This decision did not mean, however, that a local authority was legally unable to pay their employees an allowance of 2s. 6d. a week for each child, in addition to basic salaries and a cost of living bonus, in order to meet the increased cost of living.[2] On the other hand, in *Magrath's* case local authorities were warned that they must not make retrospective payments to their officials for services rendered in past years because they thought their predecessors had not paid adequate salaries. To do so, observed Lord Scrutton, "would be most prejudicial to the working of local government and unreasonable in the highest degree."[3] The legal doctrine is that since the officer has no right to claim such payments, they are mere gifts and therefore *ultra vires* the council. The power to remunerate must not be interpreted to include the power to make gifts.

Broadly speaking local authorities have been left free to determine the remuneration of their employees as they think fit, subject to the legal principles referred to in these cases. In effect they must keep their wage and salary scales not substantially above the rates prevailing in the labour market. In a few instances, however, a central department can exercise a decisive influence in determining salary scales. A conspicuous example is the payment of teachers in municipal schools. The grant-in-aid of educational expenditure for long enabled the Ministry of Education to induce local authorities to observe the Burnham scales as a condition of receiving the grant-in-aid. The Education Act, 1944 authorises the Minister to make an order requiring local education authorities to comply with the salary scales fixed by the representative committees which he must himself appoint for the purpose.[4] These committees are to consist of members appointed by organs representing the local education

[1] *Roberts v. Hopwood* (1925) A.C., p. 576, see *post* p. 135.
[2] *Lewis and Others v. Walker*, 60 T.L.R., p. 47.
[3] *Re Magrath* (1934) 2 K.B., p. 415.
[4] Section 89.

authorities on the one hand and teachers on the other. The Education Act, 1944 also imposes a very important restriction on local education authorities in regard to their married women teachers. Several unsuccessful efforts were made by married women teachers to persuade the Courts of law to declare illegal the discrimination shown against them by local authorities.[1] The Sex Disqualification Removal Act, 1920 proved useless as a legal safeguard owing to the curious attitude of the Court of Appeal towards married women teachers. The Education Act, 1944 now provides that no woman shall be disqualified for employment as a teacher in any county school or voluntary school, or be dismissed from such employment, by reason only of marriage.

This statute also imposes for the first time a duty on local education authorities to appoint a fit person to be their Chief Education Officer. Further, a local authority is not to appoint its Chief Education Officer without consulting the Minister of Education and in doing so is to send him a list containing the names of the persons from whom they propose to select their officer. The Minister may prohibit the appointment of any person whose name is included in this list.

In regard to tenure of office, the position is that local authorities are frequently authorised by statute to appoint officers or servants "during the pleasure of the council." It was held in the case of *Brown v. Dagenham Urban District Council* [1929] 1 K.B. 737, that where the law prescribes that the appointment shall be in these terms, a local authority could dismiss a member of their staff without notice and without cause, even though he had an agreement with the council providing that notice should be given. This harsh rule was abolished by the Local Government Act, 1933, s. 121, which provides that notwithstanding any provision in that or any other enactment that a person should hold office during the pleasure of the local authority, there may be included in the terms of appointment a provision that it shall not be terminated except upon such reasonable notice being given as may be

[1]*Short v. Poole Corporation* (1926) 1 Ch., p. 66; *Fennell v. East Ham Corporation* (1926) 1 Ch., p. 641.

agreed between the parties. Any provision of this kind is validated by the Act and is legally enforceable.

A comprehensive pension scheme is essential in the public service and for many years local government failed to provide this. The problem was dealt with piecemeal by legislation authorising superannuation schemes for particular classes of officials such as poor law officers,[1] asylums officers,[2] fire brigade officers,[3] police officers,[4] and school teachers.[5] In 1922 any local authority was empowered, it if wished, to adopt a general superannuation scheme for all its officers.[6] Many local authorities did not take advantage of this statute and for this reason mobility within the service was restricted. The Local Government Superannuation Act, 1937 effected a great improvement by making superannuation compulsory and universal throughout local government.

The terms and conditions of employment of local government officers and workmen have been profoundly affected by the growth of Whitley Councils. Of particular importance is the Scheme of Conditions of Service agreed by the National Joint Council for Local Authorities' Administrative, Professional, Technical and Clerical Services. This scheme, which is generally known as the Local Government Officers' Charter, deals with a wide variety of matters including recruitment and training, hours of work, annual and special leave, discipline, sickness payments, removal expenses, salary scales, promotion, official conduct, and so forth. It has been almost universally adopted by local authorities throughout the country and must therefore be regarded as a collective agreement which (where appropriate) has been incorporated into the terms and conditions of employment of the classes of officers to which it applies.

---

[1]Poor Law Officers' Superannuation Act, 1896 (now repealed subject to preservation of existing superannuation rights).

[2]Asylums Officers' Superannuation Act, 1909 and Asylums and Certified Institutions (Officers' Pensions) Act, 1918.

[3]Fire Brigade Pensions Acts, 1925-1939.

[4]Police Pensions Act, 1921.

[5]Elementary School Teachers' (Superannuation) Act, 1898, and Teachers' (Superannuation) Acts, 1925 and 1937.

[6]Local Government and Other Officers' Superannuation Act, 1922.

For the first time conditions of service have been unified among a very high proportion of local government officers.

One other significant development which has taken place recently is the control exercised by central departments over officers serving local authorities. The chief example of this is the Food Executive Officer, who is the chief officer of the Food Control Committee. This Committee is appointed by the local authority (subject to the prior approval of the Divisional Food Officer of the Ministry of Food) to act for its area but the Committee does not report to the local authority nor is it in any way responsible to the council for its actions. The Minister of Food exercises strict control over the Committee, and the Clerk of the local authority must submit each year a list of the members of the Committee for the next ensuing year for the Minister's approval. If the Minister so directs, the appointing authority must remove any member of the Committee. The Minister must also approve any sub-committee and the work assigned to it. The Food Executive Officer is a civil servant appointed by the Minister of Food. At the outbreak of war in 1939 almost all the Food Executive Officers were Town Clerks or the Clerks to Urban and Rural District Councils. They received an honorarium and acted in a more or less consultative capacity, especially in enforcement and legal matters, to the Food Control Committee. The administration of the Food Office was mainly carried on by the Deputy Food Executive Officer, who was a full-time salaried official of the Ministry. In recent years many of these local government officers resigned their appointments and were replaced by full time salaried Food Executive Officers.

It can be seen that the Food Executive Officer was during the war acting in a dual capacity similar to that so frequently found in continental countries, where it has had adverse effects on local government. The Town Clerk who was also Food Executive Officer was receiving his instructions in regard to food control from the Minister of Food and not from the local authority. This was analogous to the situation which existed in Germany under the Weimar Constitution whereby local officials were called upon to serve two masters: the local authority in respect of municipal services and the State authority in respect of State functions. This led to a conflict of loyalty and to the official being partly independent of the local authority, with ensuing detriment to the power and status of the elected council. The present position in regard to the Food Executive Officer is changing now that most of the Food Executive Officers are civil servants,[1] but the undesirable features of the system still obtain in regard to local fuel overseers.

Local authorities are required by the Coal Distribution Order[2] to appoint a local Fuel Overseer for their areas. The appointment and removal of the officer is at the discretion of the local authority but if the Minister considers that the officer who has been appointed is unsuited to administer the Retail Coal Prices Order, 1941, he may so inform the local authority which shall forthwith remove him. The local authority may, subject to any direction from the Minister, arrange to supervise the local Fuel Overseer and they are in any event required to appoint an advisory committee to assist him. The Coal Distribution Order contains a large number of provisions which empower the Minister to give directions about the distribution of coal which are to be carried out by the local Fuel Overseer. The local Fuel Overseer is legally obliged to carry out these requirements without reference to the local authority and with no responsibility towards them. Moreover the Minister is expressly authorised by the Order to give such directions as he thinks fit to the local Fuel Overseer appertaining to the exercise of the powers conferred and duties imposed on him by the Order and as to the forms which he is to use for this purpose. Anyone who is aggrieved by any action of a local Fuel Overseer is to appeal not to the local authority but to the Regional Coal Officer of the Ministry of Fuel and Power.

By these provisions the Minister is given direct authority over senior officers of local authorities acting in their capacity as local Fuel Overseers. This is something new in English local government. It is, in the writer's opinion, deplorable that we

[1] On October 1st, 1948, there were 756 Food Executive Officers who were full-time salaried officers of the Ministry of Food as compared with 406 part-time Food Executive Officers who were also local government officers.

[2] S.R. & O. 1138/1945.

108

should have adopted a feature which is typical of many foreign systems of local government which are inferior from a democratic point of view to that which has hitherto existed in Britain for more than a hundred years. It is one aspect of the tendency towards centralisation which is an outstanding feature of recent developments in the British system of government.

6. ADMINISTRATIVE POWERS

We may now turn to the difficult and complex topic of administrative powers.

Everyone is conscious of the fact that the powers of public authorities have increased enormously during the past 30 years. Yet it is exceedingly difficult to present this indisputable tendency in terms of administrative law, for the simple reason that scarcely any work has been done on the subject in Britain. We have no English counterpart of the late Professor Freund's *Administrative Powers over Persons and Property*[1]. Vague accusations and denunciation are a poor substitute for scientific analysis, classification and generalisation. In consequence, the most severe critics of the growth of executive power have contributed little or nothing to our understanding of the problem. What we need is an analysis of the main types of administrative powers which exist in various fields of administrative action with an examination of the extent to which they have been used in practice. It might then be possible to compare the powers conferred on different authorities, or on the same authorities in connection with different functions, with the object of discovering how far the marked diversities of legislative practice which exist are the result of genuine differences of need or are due to mere habit or historic accident. By this means we might hope gradually to construct a rational basis for the formulation of administrative powers which would enable us to avoid conferring excessive powers on public authorities (by which I mean powers in excess of their proved needs); which would eliminate or at least discourage the more arbitrary or irresponsible forms now in use; and which would encourage the use

[1]University of Chicago Press, 1928.

by Ministers, Parliamentary Counsel and Members of Parliament of the more satisfactory legislative expressions.

Only by some such process can we hope to effect real improvement in the position. Looking back over the past thirty years we are forced to recognise that in this branch of administrative law the greatest growth has taken place and the greatest chaos has been permitted to occur. I can do no more here than to indicate a few significant aspects of the general trends.

The principal additions to administrative power have taken place in connection with the newer functions of government. Until 1939 there was no control of food distribution and no Ministry of Food. Almost the only powers which public authorities exercised were those conferred by the Food and Drugs Acts or cognate legislation intended to promote hygiene. To-day there is a vast network of regulation which controls producers, manufacturers, processers, wholesalers, retailers and consumers of food. The same is true of clothing, coal and petrol. The rationing or restriction of articles of common consumption, and the regulation of prices, inevitably involves a vast extension of administrative powers over persons and property.

Take, again, town and country planning. In 1920 there was only some rudimentary legislation on the statute book which applied to the unbuilt portions of towns; in practice this was almost ignored. To-day, control over land use covers every part of the country, whether urban or rural. It directly affects every landowner and every person who wishes to develop the use of land. Stringent duties and liabilities have been placed on private interests and local planning authorities, while at the centre there is a Ministry of Town and Country Planning aided by the Central Land Board. It would be impossible to achieve a radical transformation of this kind without very large extensions of administrative power. One could go through the whole range of public and social services in similar manner, indicating extensions or additions of power to correspond to the enlarged scope of governmental functions.

We may note in passing that although it is often said that the rise of the social service state is the leading characteristic of the 20th century, many of the most important modern functions of Government consist of regulatory powers (i.e. those which control the conduct of citizens) rather than of service powers (i.e. those where the Government provides a service for the public). It is, moreover, the regulatory activities of Government which bear most hardly upon the public. It is here that the conflict of public and private interest can become most vexatious and widespread. If, for example, the Ministry of Health and local authorities are given powers to build or repair shops and factories, the result may affect the taxpayer but he is unlikely to have any very strong or lasting feeling of vexation about it. On the other hand, a restriction on the building or repair of shops or factories by private firms or companies will easily give rise to a keen sense of resentment, injustice and frustration which will probably not be confined to the interests directly affected.

A conspicuous feature of the period under review has been the emergence of powers formulated in what are known as subjective terms. Until recently it was customary to confer statutory powers on public authorities in terms which provided that they should have a right to take action of a specified kind in the event of certain defined conditions being satisfied. The existence of the specified conditions must then be established before the authority is legally entitled to act. While a public authority may *assume* that the conditions precedent have been satisfied and will usually act on that assumption, its action can always be challenged in the Courts on the ground that the required conditions have not in fact been fulfilled and that in consequence it was not authorised to act. This is sometimes referred to as a question of jurisdictional fact because it relates to the facts on which the jurisdiction of the authority is based.

For example, the Food and Drugs Act, 1938, section 12, provides that "if an authorised officer of a local authority has reason to suspect that any cart, barrow or other vehicle, or any container, contains any food intended for sale for human consumption or in the course of delivery after sale for human consumption, he may examine the contents of the vehicle, or, as the case may be, of the container, and for that purpose may, if necessary, detain the vehicle or the container, and, if he finds any food which appears to him to be intended for, but unfit for, human consumption" he may deal with it in the manner laid down elsewhere in the Act.

The powers here given to a sanitary inspector are formulated in terms which enable his action to be reviewed by a Court. The question whether the inspector had "reason" to suspect that a vehicle contains food for human consumption is liable to be tested by the light of "public" reason, not according to the officer's private opinion. The question whether it is "necessary" to detain the vehicle or container in order to examine the contents is, again, not a matter to be determined finally and exclusively by the officer but one on which the Court can make up its mind in a case where wrongful detention of the goods is alleged. Even the language employed in regard to the condition of the foodstuff does not give the inspector a right to determine the liability of the seller. It merely enables him to seize the foodstuff which "appears to him" to be unsound and to remove it in order to have it dealt with by a justice of the peace.

In recent years Parliament has passed much legislation which states that where a Minister is satisfied that certain facts exist, or where it appears to him that something has occurred or is required, he can thereupon exercise the powers specified in the enactment. There are several examples of this in the Agriculture Act, 1947. Thus, by Section 12 (1) "Where the Minister of Agriculture and Fisheries . . . is satisfied that the owner of agriculture land is not fulfilling his responsibilities to manage the land in accordance with the rule of good estate management, or that the occupier of an agricultural unit is not fulfilling his responsibilities to farm the unit in accordance with the rules of good husbandry" the Minister may make an order placing the owner or occupier as the case may be under his supervision as regards the management of the land in the former instance or the farming of the unit in the latter. While a supervision order is in force the Minister has extensive powers of direction and dispossession conferred by Part II of the Act.[1]

[1] See also Section 84(1) of the Agriculture Act, 1947; also Town and Country Planning Act, 1947, Section 39(1).

Enabling powers formulated in subjective terms have been liberally conferred on the new public corporations established to operate socialised industries. The Coal Industry Nationalisation Act, 1946 declares that the National Coal Board shall have power to do any thing and to enter into any transaction which "in their opinion" is calculated to facilitate the proper discharge of their statutory duties.[1] The functions of the Board include the carrying on of all such activities "as it may appear to the Board to be requisite, advantageous or convenient for them to carry on for or in connection with the discharge of their duties. . . ."[2] It would, I believe, be exceedingly difficult, if not impossible, to persuade a Court to declare any act of the Board *ultra vires* if it involved substituting the Court's own opinion for the opinion of the Board as to its being necessary, or advantageous or convenient.[3]

The legal effect of powers formulated in subjective terms has been considered by the Courts in a number of cases during the past ten years. The case which attracted most attention was *Liversidge v. Anderson* (1942) A.C. 206, which went to the House of Lords. This was one of a series of cases which arose under Defence Regulation 18B. This provided that if the Home Secretary "has reasonable cause to believe any person to be of hostile origin or associations, or to have been recently concerned in acts prejudicial to the public safety or the defence of the realm, or in the preparation or instigation of such acts, and that by reason thereof it is necessary to exercise control over him," he could make an order against that person directing that he be detained. The question on which the action turned was whether the decision of the Home Secretary could be reviewed by a Court of law to enquire whether he had a reasonable cause to arrive at a belief concerning a particular detainee; or whether the validity of an order depended solely on the belief, whether ill-founded or well-founded, in the Minister's mind. In short, did the regulation mean that the Home Secretary must have such cause for his belief as a Court of law would hold to be sufficient to induce belief in the mind

[1]Section 1 (3).   [2]Section 1 (2).
[3]Not all the Corporations are given powers in subjective terms. See for examples to the contrary, the Civil Aviation Act, 1946 and the New Towns Act, 1946.

of any ordinary reasonable man, or did it mean that he need have only such cause of belief as he himself deemed to be reasonable? As Lord Macmillan pointed out, to require that a cause of belief shall be reasonable implies a reference to some standard of reasonableness. Was the standard of reasonableness to be satisfied an impersonal standard independent of the Home Secretary's own mind, or was it the personal standard of what the Home Secretary himself deemed reasonable? A world of difference would result from these two interpretations of the regulation. "In the former case," Lord Macmillian explained, "the reasonableness of the cause which the Secretary of State had for his belief may, if challenged, be examined by a court of law in order to determine whether he had such cause of belief as would satisfy the ordinary reasonable man, and to enable the court to adjudicate on this question there must be disclosed to it the facts and circumstance which the Secretary of State had before him in arriving at his belief. In the latter case it is for the Secretary of State alone to decide in the forum of his own conscience whether he has a reasonable cause of belief, and he cannot, if he has acted in good faith, be called on to disclose to anyone the facts and circumstances which have induced his belief or to satisfy anyone but himself that these facts and circumstances constituted a reasonable cause of belief."[1]

A majority of the Law Lords decided that it was for the Home Secretary alone to decide whether he had reasonable cause to believe that the conditions under Regulation 18B had been satisfied. The highest tribunal held that there was no triable issue as to reasonableness under Regulation 18B, and no court could consider whether the administrative discretion vested in the Home Secretary had been properly exercised.

Lord Atkin delivered a powerful dissenting speech which has often been quoted, as much for its insistence on legal principle in time of national danger as for the lucidity of its expression.

It was not surprising, after this decision, that where a Defence Regulation authorised the Government to take control of an undertaking "if it appears to a competent authority that it was

[1]*Liversidge v. Anderson* (1942) A.C. 206, at pp. 247-248.

necessary to do so" in the interests of the public safety, the defence of the realm, or the efficient prosecution of the war, or for maintaining supplies and services essential to the life of the community, the court should decide that it has no jurisdiction to interfere with a *bona fide* decision by the Minister within his delegated authority. In the *Point of Ayr Colliery case* the appellants, a colliery company, contended that there were no adequate grounds upon which the Minister could arrive at the conclusion at which he had arrived in order to take over the colliery, but the Court of Appeal would not listen to this argument. "If one thing is settled beyond the possibility of dispute," said Lord Greene, the Master of the Rolls, "it is that, in construing regulations of this character expressed in this particular form of language, it is for the competent authority, whatever Ministry that may be, to decide as to whether or not a case for the exercise of the powers has arisen. If is for the competent authority to judge of the adequacy of the evidence before it. It is for the competent authority to judge of the credibility of that evidence. It is for the competent authority to judge whether or not it is desirable or necessary to make further investigations and perhaps negotiation. All those matters are placed by Parliament in the hands of the Minister in the belief that the Minister will exercise his powers properly, and in the knowledge that, if he does not do so, he is liable to the criticism of Parliament. One thing is certain, and that is that those matters are not within the competence of this court. It is the competent authority that is selected by Parliament to come to the decision, and, if that decision is come to in good faith, this court has no power to interfere, provided, of course, that the action is one which is within the four corners of the authority delegated to the Minister.

"In my opinion the appellants' evidence does not establish any circumstances which gives this court power to interfere with what is admittedly the *bona fide* decision of the Minister. We cannot investigate the adequacy of his reasons. We cannot investigate the rapidity or the lack of investigation, if it existed, with which he acted. We cannot investigate any of those things because Parliament in its decision has withdrawn those matters

from the courts and has entrusted them to the Ministers concerned, the constitutional safeguard being, as I have said, the
supervision of Ministers exercised by Parliament: that being so,
that is an end of the case."[1]

So far we have been dealing with cases arising under Defence
Regulations which were passed to deal with a national
emergency of the gravest possible character. While the courts
were not apparently influenced by the existence of the
emergency, they did take account of it as an indication, as
Lord Macmillan explained in *Liversidge v. Anderson*, that a
regulation for the defence of the realm might quite properly
have a meaning which, because of its drastic invasion of the
liberty of the subject, the courts would be slow to attribute to a
peace-time measure.[2] But in some actions which were brought
in 1947 against the Minister of Town and Country Planning,
it was held that legislation in that more peaceful sphere could
possess similar legal attributes.[3]

In the field of local government we shall also find a significant
development relating to administrative powers.

In 1920, it was broadly true to say that local authorities of all
classes had their powers conferred upon them direct by Act of
Parliament, supplemented, in the case of municipal corporations, by provisions contained in their charters. A few instances
could be found where local authorities could delegate functions[4];
but this was a rare occurrence which had little practicable
importance. To-day, the principle of delegation has become a
conspicuous feature of local government in the counties.

Thus, county councils are required to delegate functions to
divisional executives and excepted districts under the Education
Act, 1944;[5] and elaborate schemes of delegation have been
brought into operation in most counties. Under the Town and

---

[1] *Point of Ayr Collieries Ltd. v. Lloyd-George* (1943) 2 A.E.R. 546, at p. 547; see also
Carltona Ltd. v. Commissioners of Works and Others (1943) 2 A.E.R. 560, at p. 563.
[2] *Liversidge v. Anderson* (1942) A.C. 206, at p. 252.
[3] *Franklin and Others v. Minister of Town & Country Planning* (1947) 63 T.L.R.,
p. 446 (H.L.); see also *Robinson and Others v. Minister of Town & Country Planning*
(1947) 63 T.L.R., 374 C.A. Also re *Beck and Pollitzer's application* (1948) 2 K.B. 339.
[4] E.g. Local Government Act 1888, Section 28 (2); Local Government Act 1894,
Section 15.
[5] 1st Schedule, Part III, 2.

Country Planning Act, 1947,[1] regulations may be (and have been)[2] made by the Minister authorising or requiring local planning authorities to delegate to county district councils in their areas any of their functions under Part III of the Act, which deals with control of development.

The effect of these powers is to introduce a hierarchical element into our system of local government which it did not previously possess. The county council becomes the controlling authority for policy, planning and finance (subject to the overriding powers of the relevant Minister) while the county district council or the divisional executive (which always contains a large number of county district councillors) assumes a subordinate position as the administrative body for carrying out the policy laid down by the County Council.

7. DELEGATED LEGISLATION

The practice of delegating legislative powers to the Executive began centuries ago. It was firmly established and extensively used long before administrative law was ever heard of in England. Nevertheless, the proliferation of Defence of the Realm regulations during the war of 1914-18 led to an outcry not only against these regulations but against the practice of delegation itself. The report of the Committee on Ministers' Powers was in general favourable to the principle of delegation, subject to certain qualifications and safeguards. The Committee explained clearly and forcibly the need for delegation and set limits to the practice which are both reasonable and practicable. Their most important recommendations were to the effect that the precise limits of the law-making power conferred by Parliament on a Minister should always be expressly defined in clear language by the statute which confers it; and that the so-called Henry VIII clause should not be used save in exceptional circumstances and should be explained in a ministerial memorandum attached to the Bill. The jurisdiction of the courts to enquire into the legal validity of a statutory instrument should not be excluded save in the most exceptional cases; and where this is proposed in a Bill the reasons for it should be set out in a

[1]Section 34 (1).　[2]S.R. and O. 1947, No. 2499.

ministerial memorandum attached to the Bill. In such cases
Parliament should make its intention unmistakably clear
in the statute and even then the Committee considered that
there should be at least a short period of three to six months
during which the right of challenge in the courts could be
claimed. The Committee recommended that the departmental
practice of attaching to certain regulations or rules a note
explaining the changes effected thereby should be extended.
They viewed with approval the practice of departments consulting organisations interested in regulations which are being
drafted by the department concerned. They made proposals for
a Standing Committee to be set up in each House of Parliament
for the purpose of scrutinising Bills delegating legislative powers
to Ministers and for considering and reporting on regulations
made in the exercise of such powers.

No steps were taken in regard to the setting up of Parliamentary Committees to scrutinise delegated legislation until 1944, but
there was a continuous effort made by a group of back-bench
Members of Parliament to keep the subject in the foreground of
public interest and Parliamentary attention; and the spate of
statutory instruments issued during the war of 1939-1945 helped
to lend force to their contention that a greater degree of Parliamentary supervision was needed than had hitherto existed.

On the 19th January, 1943, Mr. Herbert Morrison, the
Home Secretary, stated in the House of Commons that new
Defence Regulations which are difficult to understand without
some knowledge of matters which cannot be made apparent on
the face of the regulation, would in future be accompanied by
an explanatory note or memorandum. The practice was then
instituted of printing short explanatory memoranda as footnotes
to the Statutory Rules and Orders in which new Defence
Regulations are embodied. A few months later, in May 1943
after a further debate in the House of Commons, the Home
Secretary announced that the practice of appending explanatory notes to Defence Regulations would be extended to cover
departmental orders and other subordinate instruments made
under the Defence Regulations, and that the practice should be
developed to the fullest possible extent. These explanatory

notes are intended only to enable the reader to understand the meaning of the statutory instrument. They are in no sense a legal interpretation thereof, since that is a function of the courts and not of Ministers. Nor are they a defence of the Governmental policy embodied in the instrument.

A further advance was made in the course of a long debate which took place a year later, on 17th May, 1944, when Mr. Hugh Molson moved the setting up of "a Select Committee, with power to send for persons, papers or records, whose duty it should be to carry on a continuous examination of all Statutory Rules and Orders and other instruments of Delegated Legislation presented to Parliament; and to report from week to week whether in the Committee's opinion any such instrument is obscure or contains matter of a controversial nature or should for any other reason be brought to the special attention of the House."

Mr. Morrison, who was still Home Secretary, reviewed the steps which the Government had already taken for providing necessary explanations of Defence Regulations and subordinate orders and other matters of a similar kind, and he said that the question now raised was whether some new and further check could be introduced to regulate the exercise of legislative powers by the Executive. He regarded this as a fair request.

The Coalition Government then accepted the establishment of a scrutinising committee such as the Committee on Ministers' Powers had proposed, though with more restricted functions. The Home Secretary emphasised the need to limit the size of the Select Committee in order that it should not become a debating assembly and thus unable to maintain "that high judicial spirit which everybody has urged it should endeavour to do."[1] The function of the Select Committee was expressly declared to be the protection of the authority of Parliament and not the furtherance of the interests of any particular party or group.

At this point Mr. Morrison explained that Ministers would not appear before the Committee, but that officials from the departments could go in order to give technical or other background information and to answer questions. He even laid it down that the Committee should not draw the special attention

[1] See Debate on 26th May, 1943. *Hansard*, Vol. 389, Col. 1593.

of the House to a regulation unless it had either heard an officer of the department concerned or seen a departmental memorandum on the subject. (This was not to include access to the official files or disclosure of the advice given by civil servants to their political chief.)

This part of the Home Secretary's statement was a remarkable concession, since it went beyond the resolution which Mr. Molson had moved.

On the 21st June, 1944, the House of Commons ordered:[1]

That a Select Committee be appointed to consider every Statutory Rule or Order (including any Provisional Rule made under s. 2 of the Rules Publication Act, 1893) laid or laid in draft before the House, being a Rule, Order or Draft upon which proceedings may be or might have been taken in either House, in pursuance of any Act of Parliament, with a view to determining whether the special attention of the House should be drawn to it on any of the following grounds:—

(i) that it imposes a charge on the public revenues or contains provisions requiring payment to be made to the Exchequer or any Government department or to any local or public authority in consideration of any licence or consent, or of any services to be rendered, or prescribes the amount of any such charge or payments;

(ii) that it is made in pursuance of an enactment containing specific provisions excluding it from challenge in the courts, either at all times or after the expiration of a specified period;

(iii) that it appears to make some unusual or unexpected use of the powers conferred by the statute under which it is made;

(iv) that it purports to have retrospective effect where the parent statute confers no express authority so to provide;

(v) that there appears to have been unjustifiable delay in the publication or in the laying of it before Parliament;

(vi) that there appears to have been unjustifiable delay in sending a notification to Mr. Speaker under the proviso to subsection (1) of section four of the Statutory Instruments Act, 1946, where an Instrument has come into operation before it has been laid before Parliament.

[1] The terms of reference of the Select Committee were amended subsequently and are given in their revised form.

(vii) that for any special reason, its form or purport calls for elucidation.

It was further ordered that the Committee should have the assistance of the Counsel to the Speaker; that it could sit during any adjournment of the House; that it can require any Government department to submit a memorandum or to depute a representative to appear before it to explain any such Rule, Order or Draft; and that the Committee should not draw the attention of the House to any Rule, Order or Draft before affording an opportunity of this kind to the Government department concerned.

The Committee got to work rapidly and issued a number of brief reports at short intervals. These reports set out the Rules or Orders which the Committee had scrutinised and then stated either that the Committee were of opinion that there were no reasons for drawing the special attention of the House to them on any of the grounds set out in the terms of reference; or alternatively that the Committee considered that one or more of the Rules or Orders were objectionable on grounds which the report specified. It is usual for the Committee to print any memorandum or other communication submitted to it by the relevant department.

In addition to its ordinary reports, the Committee also publishes Special Reports. The ordinary reports relate to specific Statutory Rules and Orders, while the Special Reports deal with general principles or practice not related to a particular Statutory Rule and Order, although particular examples are often quoted by way of illustration.

One of the most interesting devices for controlling the exercise of legislative powers delegated to Ministers is to be found in the National Insurance Act, 1946. The Act requires the Minister of National Insurance to appoint an Advisory Committee and to submit to it preliminary drafts of nearly all the many regulations which he is authorised to make. The Committee must give public notice that it has received the preliminary draft and fix a period during which objections to the draft can be made to it by any person or body affected by the regulation. The Committee may, if it thinks fit, take oral evidence both from objectors and from representatives of the department; it can also itself raise objections on any aspect of the preliminary draft. After considering the preliminary draft and any objections, the Committee reports to the Minister, who must consider the report. The Minister then makes the regulation or lays a draft of it before Parliament, either in its original form or as amended, together with the Committee's report. If the Minister does not accept any change proposed by the Committee, he must explain to Parliament in a written statement the reasons which have led him to reject it.[1]

Here we have a new institutional device for scrutinising regulations which may prove to be of great significance. The Committee is non-political and impartial. Its members either already possess or will acquire special knowledge of the intricacies of social insurance. Their statutory duty is to advise and assist the Minister, but their true function would seem to lie in holding the balance between the administrative needs of the department and the interests of the public. This experiment may ultimately be found to contain the germs of a solution of the problem of delegated legislation.[2]

The Advisory Committee's task in no sense duplicates or renders unnecessary the task of the Select Committee on Statutory Instruments. The latter body is concerned with constitutional propriety and Parliamentary usage but not with policy or merits. The former Committee, on the other hand, may consider both administrative policy and merits but would not usually be concerned with the Parliamentary or constitutional aspects of regulations.[3]

[1] National Insurance Act 1946, Sections 41, 77 and Fifth Schedule.
[2] The forerunner of the National Insurance Advisory Committee was the Unemployment Insurance Statutory Committee, set up by the Unemployment Act 1933. But the functions of that Committee related primarily to maintaining the solvency of the Unemployment Insurance Scheme, and although it had somewhat similar powers to the present Advisory Committee in regard to regulations, they were in practice of far less importance owing to the fact that comparatively few regulations came before it. The National Insurance Act 1946, leaves to regulations many matters which in the earlier schemes were dealt with by statutory enactment. See Sir W. Beveridge: *The Unemployment Insurance Statutory Committee* (published by the London School of Economics and Political Science).
[3] See Hugh Molson, M.P.: *Delegated Legislation*, Hansard Society Pamphlet.

An important aspect of delegated legislation concerns the method of conferring powers on local authorities. Before 1919, local authorities derived their powers from public and private Acts of Parliament and, in the case of boroughs, from their charters. The provisional order was introduced in the latter half of the 19th century as a method whereby Government departments were authorised to make orders conferring powers on local authorities. The Tramways Act, 1870, the Public Health Act, 1875, and the Local Government Act, 1888, enabled departmental orders of this kind to be made. Provisional orders must, in order to become legally valid, be incorporated in a Provisional Order Confirmation Bill which is presented to Parliament by the Minister concerned. The method is much cheaper and more efficient than the private Bill procedure which it was designed to supersede in certain spheres.

In 1919, further legislative powers were delegated to the Executive. The Electricity Supply Act of that year enabled orders embodying the schemes settled by the Electricity Commissioners to be confirmed by the Board of Trade (later the Minister of Transport) and to take effect when approved by a resolution of each House of Parliament. This procedure involved the delegation to the Minister of further important aspects of the legislative process, leaving only the first stage (i.e. the authorisation of the order by the Act) and the final stage of the positive resolution, to be carried out in the Parliamentary forum. This procedure by special order has been applied to many administrative matters, such as changes in the speed limit for motor cars, the highway code, and orders raising the rate of import duty levied under a statute.

A later phase which has been reached in the process of delegating legislative power is to be found in the scheme. Here we have an arrangement whereby local authorities are required or authorised to prepare and submit to the appropriate central department, schemes for the administration or development of their work in some particular sphere of activity. A scheme so submitted may usually be approved, modified or rejected by the Minister. An approved scheme must sometimes be laid before Parliament by the appropriate Minister and is there subject either to a negative or a positive resolution. After having survived Parliamentary scrutiny—if any—the scheme then takes effect in the locality to which it applies with the force of law. It has a binding effect both on the local authority or other body concerned, and also on private persons or outside interests.

The scheme method has been widely used in connection with public assistance, housing and slum clearance, public health, education, town and country planning and other spheres of administration. The Education Act, 1944, for example, required every local education authority to estimate the immediate and prospective needs of its area in regard to primary and secondary education. Within a specified time the authority was obliged to prepare and submit to the Minister of Education a development plan showing the action which the authority proposed should be taken for securing that there shall be sufficient primary and secondary schools available for their area, and the successive measures by which that aim is to be accomplished. Section 11 of the Act, which lays this obligation on local education authorities, also specifies in considerable detail the particular matters which are to be dealt with in the development plan. It also describes the various persons who are to be consulted by the local education authority before submitting their development plan to the Minister. The Minister then considers any objections which are made to him within a period of two months, and after introducing any modifications in the plan which he considers necessary or expedient after consulting with the local education authority, the Minister is to approve the plan.

By Section 12 of the Education Act, after the Minister has approved the development plan, he makes a local education order specifying the county and voluntary schools which the authority has the duty to maintain. The order also defines the duties of the local education authority respecting the measures they are to take for securing sufficient primary and secondary schools in their area and for classifying maintained or assisted schools. If the local education authority inform the Minister that they are aggrieved by his order or by any amendment of it which he may subsequently make, the order or the amendment is to be laid before Parliament and is there subject to a negative resolution in either House of Parliament.

The advantages of the scheme method are that it combines the full use of local initiative and local knowledge with an adequate degree of central supervision and the protection of third parties whose interests may be injuriously affected. A duty is placed on the local authority to initiate the preparation of a scheme, and they are given a very large degree of freedom in formulating their proposals. The Minister's function is to act as a clearing house of information, to provide technical advice, to see that a minimum standard of achievement and progress is attained and to prevent the local authority from trampling unjustly on private interests or possibly the interests of neighbouring authorities. The role of Parliament has been immensely reduced. It is confined in the first place to enacting the statutory obligation to prepare and submit a scheme; and in the last place to approving by a negative or positive resolution the scheme which the Minister has submitted. But this last phase is omitted in the case of the local health plans which are called for under the National Health Service Act, 1946; and in the case of school development plans the sanction of Parliament is sought only if the local education order fails to satisfy the local education authority.[1]

8. Administrative Justice

The modern movement towards conferring judicial functions on Government departments or on tribunals controlled directly or indirectly, or appointed by, Ministers of the Crown, began about 70 years ago. It originated mainly in social legislation, such as the Public Health Act, 1875, but one powerful stream of tendency flowed through the successive Railway and Canal Commissions which were set up to regulate the railways in 1873 and 1888. By 1920 judicial functions had been conferred on a wide variety of administrative tribunals such as the Minister of Health, the Board of Trade, the Ministry (then the Board) of Education, the District Auditor, the Home Secretary, the Electricity Commission, the Courts of Referees, the London

[1] See also the Statutory Orders (Special Procedure) Act, 1945, and the Statutory Instruments Act, 1946.

Building Tribunal, the Registrar of Friendly Societies, the pension appeal bodies and several others. Their jurisdiction covered an extensive range of subjects, including public health, housing, education, unemployment insurance, health insurance, pensions of all kinds, local government, trade unions, public utilities and numerous other matters.

By 1930 politicians, officials, lawyers and political scientists had become aware of this movement. It had been described, interpreted, misinterpreted, defended and denounced. Shadows of the Star Chamber began to stalk the land. It was in these circumstances that in 1929 the Committee on Ministers' Powers was appointed to consider "the powers exercised by or under the direction of (or by persons or bodies appointed specially by) Ministers of the Crown by way of (a) delegated legislation and (b) judicial or quasi-judicial decision, and to report what safeguards are desirable or necessary to secure the constitutional principles of the sovereignty of Parliament and the supremacy of the Law."

It is neither possible nor necessary to review here the Committee's conclusions on administrative justice. The tone of the report was sane and temperate. This, indeed, was one of its chief merits. As I have written elsewhere: "Ghosts were laid which have not subsequently stalked the corridors of even the most orthodox constitutional lawyers. The cloak and dagger view of bureaucratic conspiracy faded quietly away."[1] Unfortunately, however, the Committee was so restricted by its own narrow ideas about the rule of law that it failed to make any practicable proposals, except on matters of procedure, for the reform of administrative justice. It failed to produce a practicable criterion by which judicial functions should be entrusted to Ministers and administrative tribunals. It rejected my proposals for a system of administrative courts. Above all, it allowed itself to be hamstrung by the illusory distinction between judicial and quasi-judicial decisions which was contained in the Committee's terms of reference and introduced in many different forms by several witnesses, notably the

[1] See my *Justice and Administrative Law* (2nd revised edition), Stevens, 1947, p. 374. This book deals with the whole question of administrative justice at full length.

Treasury Solicitor. The Committee's purpose in pursuing this chimerical distinction was to recommend that judicial decisions should normally be confided to the Courts while quasi-judicial decisions can properly be entrusted to administrative tribunals.

In the 17 years which have elapsed since the Committee reported in 1932 there has been a substantial further development of administrative justice. The National Service Acts, the Education Act, 1944, the Town and Country Planning Acts, the National Insurance, Act, 1946, and the National Insurance (Industrial Injuries) Act, 1946, the Transport Act, 1947, the Reinstatement in Civil Employment Act, 1944, the Family Allowances Act, 1945, the Agricultural Act, 1947, and many other measures have increased the number, enlarged the jurisdiction, and raised the status of administrative tribunals. Among the most significant items in this great extension are the substitution of administrative tribunals under the new national insurance scheme for industrial injury claims in place of the jurisdiction of the Courts in workmen's compensation cases; and the creation of administrative tribunals to deal with the rent of furnished dwellings. The Report of the Committee on Ministers' Powers has had little or no influence on the course of events in this sphere.

The development of administrative justice has been disorderly and unsystematic in the period under review, but we can nevertheless discern certain emerging trends. The most conspicuous is the adoption of the three-man tribunal as the typical body for dispensing administrative justice. We find this type adopted for the discharge of judicial functions in connection with the new national insurance schemes, the postponement of call-up for military service, reinstatement of ex-service men in civil employment, the supervision of independent schools, unemployment assistance, the control of rents for furnished dwellings, the regulation of road and rail transport and other matters. Such tribunals are usually constituted on a tripartite basis, the chairman being independent, while the other members represent special interests or possess special qualifications relevant to the questions to be determined.

While there is thus a strong tendency in several spheres to

establish specific tribunals which are clearly differentiated from the Courts of Law on the one hand and from the executive authorities responsible for administering services on the other, we find elsewhere a reversion to the older and less desirable method of conferring judicial powers—either of first instance or appellate—on a Minister *simpliciter*. This has occurred in town and country planning, education, the national medical service, police appeals and the superannuation of local government officers.

No attempt has been made to set up an Administrative Court of Appeal, but provision has been made in several instances for a superior tribunal to hear appeals in a specialised field from an administrative tribunal of first instance.

Thus the Industrial Injuries Commissioner and Deputy Commissioners (appointed by the Crown) are the final adjudicating authority on questions both of law and fact arising under the national insurance scheme for injured workpeople, except in regard to the medical aspects of industrial injuries, where an appeal lies from a medical board to a medical appeal tribunal. The National Insurance Commissioner and Deputy Commissioners are the final appellate authority for deciding appeals from the local tribunals under the general insurance scheme. There is an Umpire and Deputy Umpires to hear appeals from the Reinstatement Committees. Similar arrangements exist for appeals under the National Service Acts. But here again there is no uniformity of practice and several instances could be given where an appeal lies to a Minister.

The directions in which the least progress has been made are in the publication of decisions and in requiring administrative tribunals to give the reasons—or at least the grounds—for their decisions. In some instances there has been an actual recession in recent decades.

9. THE RELATIONS BETWEEN CENTRAL AND LOCAL GOVERN-
MENT

It is convenient to regard the relations between central and local government as a separate topic of administrative law, although they could logically be treated under the heading of administrative powers.

England differs from most unitary countries in that there has never been a single pattern of the central-local relationship extending uniformly over the whole field of local government administration. It can be said rather that each service has had its own particular type of relationship. Hence there are almost as many different kinds of relations as there are local government services. This may be a slight exaggeration; but the multiplicity and diversity of relationships are indisputable.

The relations between central and local authorities grew up in a purely empirical manner. Abstract theory and general principle played little part in the process. The problems presented by each service were dealt with as they arose; or, more often, when they were recognised to exist. In consequence there is little in common between the relations subsisting in the sphere of public assistance and those in education; or between those in public health and those in police. The aims and purposes of central intervention were different in each instance and therefore different methods were employed. In general the outstanding features of the English system of local government have been until recently the relatively large amount of freedom from domination by the central government possessed by local authorities and the correspondingly strict control exercised by Parliament and the Judiciary. Local authorities' powers were defined and limited by legislation; and these limitations were enforced by the Courts through the doctrine of *ultra vires*.[1]

In consequence we have not had anything resembling a prefecture on the French model. The Government does not have power to suspend or dissolve a local authority; nor to require it to submit its annual budget for approval.

Central control over local government has, however, increased enormously during the last 30 years. This is reflected in nearly all the principal services which local authorities now administer. It is shown even more eloquently by the fact that many of the most important functions which local authorities formerly carried out have been transferred either to central

[1]See my *Development of Local Government* (revised second edition), pp. 235-253.

departments or to public boards and corporations appointed by Ministers. Prior to 1920 the only function which had been transferred from local authorities to the central government was the prison service. But since 1930 trunk roads have been transferred to the Ministry of Transport; civil airfields to the Ministry of Civil Aviation; hospitals to the Ministry of Health; valuation and assessment of property for rating to the Inland Revenue; the provision of assistance to persons in need of relief to the National Assistance Board; the regulation of motor transport for passengers and goods to the Licensing Authorities; electricity supply to the Electricity Boards; gas undertakings to the Gas Boards; while municipally owned motorbus and trolleybus services are liable to be transferred to new bodies which may be set up under the Transport Act, 1947. This is not the place in which to comment on these changes except to point out that they form part of a general centralising movement of great strength.[1]

To go through each service in turn with the object of indicating the increase in central control which has taken place would take too much space. I shall instead take one or two services by way of illustration and then show the extent to which the principal instruments of central control have been strengthened.

The Education Act, 1944 has greatly extended the powers of the Ministry of Education over local education authorities.

The opening words of the statute declare it to be the duty of the Minister of Education "to secure the effective execution by local authorities, under his control and direction, of the national policy for providing a varied and comprehensive educational service in every area." The relationship between central and local government in the field of education has hitherto been largely a partnership, but this statement strikes a new note. It is significant that the expression "control and direction" is taken from the Poor Law Amendment Act, 1834, under which the public assistance authorities were completely subordinated to the central department.[2] Their status was described by the Court

[1] See the Prologue to my *Development of Local Government* (second revised edition, 1948) for a full discussion.
[2] Poor Law Amendment Act 1834, Section XV. Poor Law Act 1930, S. 1 (1).

of Appeal as being that of "a subordinate administrative body" performing ministerial functions as mere agents of the central department.[1] The model of 1834 has until now never been followed in any other branch of local government.

The Education Act, 1944 also breaks new ground by conferring on the Minister of Education power to prevent the "unreasonable exercise" of their functions by education authorities. The Act[2] says that if the Minister is satisfied, either on complaint by any person or otherwise, that any local education authority or the managers or governors of any county or voluntary school have acted or are proposing to act unreasonably with respect to the exercise of any power conferred or the performance of any duty imposed upon them, he may give such directions as to the exercise of the power or the performance of the duty as he thinks expedient. This over-riding provision applies even where the law expressly states that the power or duty is contingent upon the opinion of the local education authority or school managers or governors. The Minister need not wait for a complaint. He can intervene at any time.

Prior to 1938 there was no central supervision over fire brigades. The lack of interest shown by the Home Office in this essential service was, indeed, a matter for which that Department could justly be criticised. Now, however, we find that under the Fire Brigades Act, 1948,[3] very large powers have been given to the Home Office over local authorities.

The Home Secretary may make regulations governing the conditions of service of fire brigade personnel, including not only ranks, pay and allowances, but also the hours of duty and leave and the maintenance of discipline.[4] He can regulate the method of appointing the chief officers and the other members of fire brigades and determine the qualifications for promotion; and he can prescribe the promotion procedure.[5] An establish-

[1] *Tozeland v. West Ham Guardians* (1907), 1 K.B., p. 920.
[2] Section 68.
[3] During the war the fire brigades were transferred to the Ministry of Home Security. The Act of 1947 returns them to local government, though to county councils in place of county district councils.
[4] Section 17.
[5] Section 18.

ment scheme must be submitted to him by every fire authority setting out the personnel to be employed in every rank and grade, the fire stations to be maintained and the equipment to be provided. The Home Secretary may approve the scheme as submitted or with such modifications as he may direct. It then becomes binding on the local authority; and they cannot depart from it in the smallest detail without the permission of the Home Office.[1] The Act contains much else in similar vein.

Finance has played an increasingly large part in the relations between central and local government for more than a century. By 1920 grants-in-aid had come to form a large proportion of the total income of local authorities.[2] To-day the total sum received by way of grant is larger than the amount raised by rates. This has never before happened in time of peace.

In 1920 central grants took the form of assigned revenues and percentage grants for approved expenditure on specific services, such as police and education. In 1929 the Local Government Act introduced a new Block Grant. The National Exchequer Contribution, to give this grant its proper name, was a pre-determined sum distributed on the basis of the weighted population of each county and county borough calculated in accordance with a formula. It will be replaced in future by Exchequer Equalisation Grants payable under the Local Government Act, 1948.

The Act of 1929 contained a provision which for the first time gave the Minister of Health power to reduce the grant payable to a local authority by any amount he thinks fit, if he considers that the expenditure of the council has been "excessive and unreasonable" having regard to its financial resources and other relevant circumstances. He could also take similar action if he is satisfied that a local authority has "failed to achieve or maintain a reasonable standard of efficiency and progress" in its public health services, and that the health and welfare of the inhabitants of the area has been or is likely to be endangered. He

[1]Section 19.
[2]In 1921-22 local authorities received from Government grants sums amounting to £76.7 millions compared with £170.8 millions in rates and £126.6 millions from other sources such as public utility undertakings. (5th Annual Report of the Ministry of Health, 1923-4, Cmd. 2218/1924, p. 84.)

could also withhold or reduce the grant if the Minister of Transport certifies that the local authority has failed to maintain its roads in a satisfactory condition.[1] Under the new legislation these penal powers are extended so as to cover all the functions of local authorities.[2]

The only condition imposed on the Minister is that, if he decides to reduce a grant, he must lay a report of his action before Parliament. This section goes much further than was rendered necessary by the change from a system of assigned revenues and percentage grants for specified services to a block grant or an equalisation grant. Previously only a few public health services, such as the treatment of tuberculosis and venereal disease, had been grant aided and thereby made subject to a certain measure of central control. Since 1929, it has been truly said, "the whole of public health has come under indirect control operating through the Minister's power to reduce grants, and default by a local authority in carrying out one minor part of its public health duties may have very serious consequences affecting the whole of its administration."[3] In exercising these powers, the Minister could compel a local authority not merely to maintain its health services in a state which he considered efficient but actually to make progress. Moreover, by obtaining authority to penalise local councils for providing services on a basis which he considers "excessive and unreasonable," the Minister has acquired a restraining power which enables him to interfere in an entirely new way in administrative policy. The Local Government Act, 1948, generalises these Ministerial powers by allowing the Minister to reduce the new Exchequer Equalisation Grant or Exchequer Transitional Grant if he is dissatisfied with the administration of a local authority in respect of *any* of their functions.[4]

The growth of default powers is another manifestation of increasing central control during the period under review. The principle of giving a Minister legal powers to compel a recalci-

[1] Local Government Act, 1929, Section 104.
[2] Local Government Act, 1948, Section 6.
[3] *Hart's Introduction to the Law of Local Government and Administration* by W. O. Hart, (4th edition), p. 358.
[4] Section 6.

trant local authority to carry out its duties, was firmly established by the Public Health Act 1875. The earlier expressions of this power often permitted the department to make an order, enforceable in the Courts, requiring the local authority to carry out its obligatory functions; or to appoint a person to carry out the work and recoup the cost from the defaulting authority.

These comparatively mild methods of enforcing action have since given way to more stringent devices. The most drastic example was the Boards of Guardians (Default) Act, 1926, which enabled the Minister of Health to replace an elected Board of Guardians by a person or persons appointed by himself if it appeared to him that the guardians had ceased, or were acting so as to render themselves unable, to discharge all or any of their functions. This Act has been repealed but it helped to create the prevailing conception of Ministerial domination over local government.

Almost every recent statute dealing with particular services contains stringent default powers. Thus, the Public Health Act, 1936, enables the Minister, after holding a local inquiry, to declare a local authority to be in default and to direct it to perform its duty in a specified manner by a named date. If the local authority remains obdurate, he can apply to the Court for an order of mandamus. Alternatively, he can transfer the functions of a defaulting county or county borough council to himself; or of a district council to the county council. Somewhat similar powers exist in regard to housing, assistance, town and country planning and other services. The Town and Country Planning Act, 1947[1] enables the Minister, instead of himself acting in place of a local planning authority which has failed to submit satisfactory plans or proposals to him, to authorise a neighbouring planning authority to do so.

In addition to these general powers of default there are numerous instances where a Minister can act in place of a local authority in regard to a particular matter. If, for example, a local authority does not make building bye-laws which in the Minister's view are adequate, within three months of being

[1]Section 7.

required to do so by him, he can make them himself.[1] "In these matters," observes Mr. W. O. Hart, "the element of default is often slight: yet the central department is empowered itself to act if the local authority, while prepared to perform its duty, is yet not willing to perform it in a manner agreeable to the views of the department. By these methods a local authority may be forced to comply with the policy laid down by a central department. The methods of enforcement, whether through the agency of the courts, or through the action of the county council, or the central department concerned, render these default powers the most drastic form of central control yet known. . . . If these default powers are utilised, they open the door to the criticism that the system they control is not truly one of local government."[2]

One other method of control which we must notice before leaving this question is the district audit, which now covers the accounts of all local authorities except those of borough councils which are subject to the alternative systems of borough audit or professional audit. Even where the borough or professional audit is in force a considerable part of the borough council's expenditure is audited by the district auditor either for grant-in-aid purposes or for historical reasons.

The district audit originated in connection with the poor law and was extended to local government generally in the last quarter of the 19th century. During the past 30 years the auditor's powers have been greatly strengthened by legislation and judicial decision.

In *Roberts v. Hopwood* (1925) A.C., p. 576, the question before the House of Lords was the legality of a minimum wage of £4 a week paid by the Poplar Borough Council to their municipal employees from 1st May, 1920. The borough council had statutory power to pay "such salaries and wages as [they] may think fit." The District Auditor raised no objection until January 1923, when he found that the minimum wage was still being paid, although the cost of living had fallen. The £4 minimum was admittedly in excess of the wages paid under

[1] Public Health Act, 1936, Section 69.
[2] *Hart's Introduction to the Law of Local Government and Administration* by W. O. Hart (4th ed.) pp. 348-9.

collective agreements for similar work in London. The Council did not, however, take the view that wages should be exclusively related to the cost of living but that, as a matter of policy, "a public authority should be a model employer and that a minimum rate of £4 is the least wage which ought to be paid to an adult, having regard to the efficiency of the workpeople, the duty of a public authority both to the ratepayers and to its employees, the purchasing power of the wages and other considerations which are relevant to their decision as to wages."

The auditor considered the minimum wage excessive and unreasonable. He accordingly disallowed the sum of £5,000 and surcharged it upon the councillors, who appealed to the Courts. The High Court upheld the auditor but this was reversed by the Court of Appeal. The House of Lords reversed the Court of Appeal and unanimously upheld the decision of the District Auditor.

The Public Health Act, 1875, Section 247, from which the district auditor's powers were then derived, required him to disallow and surcharge every item of account "contrary to law." It was well understood that any payment which was corrupt, negligent or *ultra vires* would be contrary to law. But here the question in issue was whether expenditure of a kind which is authorised becomes illegal merely because it is "excessive" in amount. The House of Lords decided that it does. Therefore the auditor has jurisdiction to enquire into the reasonableness of every payment in terms of its amount, and to disallow any excess which is above what he considers to be reasonable. In Lord Sumner's words, "He has to restrain expenditure within proper limits. His mission is to find out if there is any excess over what is reasonable. I do not find any words limiting his functions merely to the case of bad faith, or obliging him to leave the ratepayers unprotected from the effects on their pockets of honest stupidity or unpractical idealism."[1]

The effect of this case was to make the opinion of the district auditor of what is reasonable expenditure override the views of the elected councillors, subject to a right of appeal either to the

[1] For a full discussion of the District Auditor see my *Development of Local Government* (second revised edition), Part IV.

Courts or the Minister of Health. The machinery of appeal was changed soon afterwards by the Audit (Local Authorities) Act 1927. The Act[1] provides that where a disallowance or surcharge exceeds £500, an appeal lies only to the High Court. In any other case, an aggrieved person may appeal either to the Court or to the Minister. A person who is surcharged must refund the sum to the local authority. Where the amount exceeds £500 he is also disqualified from membership of any local authority for a period of 5 years, under penalty of a fine. If the tribunal is satisfied that the person surcharged "acted reasonably or in the belief that his action was authorised by law" they may relieve him of this disqualification.

The district auditors are civil servants appointed by the Minister of Health and liable to dismissal by him. He fixes their salaries, promotes them and regulates their work. For these reasons they must be regarded as instruments of central control and therefore as forming part of the relationship between central and local government. Nevertheless, the law speaks to them directly and to this extent they are in a somewhat different position from the ordinary departmental official who exercises only the powers conferred upon his Minister.

10. JUDICIAL CONTROL OF ADMINISTRATION

I come now to the relations between the Courts of law and the Executive. The subject covers an immense ground and is exceedingly complex. For these reasons it cannot be dealt with adequately in a brief space. If one were to follow the seductive paths which lead into the labyrinth of revenue law, rating law, housing law, public health law and many other branches of administrative law, the scenery would provide many interesting vistas, but the length of the journey would be prohibitive. I can do no more here than select a few significant trends which may be regarded as fairly typical of the whole field. There is, however, a danger of over-simplification.

In considering judicial control we must distinguish between intervention by the Courts in the administrative process and the granting of a remedy for wrongful action which has already

[1] This provision was re-enacted in the local Government Act, 1933, S229.

taken place. The former may involve invalidating, quashing, or correcting the decision of a public authority, prior to action taken to carry it out. It may also involve compelling a recalcitrant authority to determine a particular matter or to take appropriate action. The declaratory order, certiorari, prohibition, mandamus and injunction are the principal instruments of judicial control of this type. In the latter type of judicial control the Court may order a public authority to redress a wrongful act which it has already committed. The remedies normally available are the payment of damages or compensation, the restitution of property wrongfully taken or detained, the abatement of a nuisance, the cessation of a continuing tort, or specific performance of a particular act. These two aspects of judicial control often merge almost imperceptibly in a single cause of action, which may result in both types of remedy being granted.

Taking first the intervention by the Courts in the administrative process, we can observe an increasing recognition of the right of public authorities to determine matters within their jurisdiction without judicial interference. In the licensing of cinemas, for example, Lord Greene, M.R., remarked that local authorities are clearly entrusted by Parliament with deciding matters which they can best deal with by virtue of their knowledge and experience. In consequence, where the licensing authority makes a decision about cinemas, or attaches conditions to a licence, the Court will confine its investigation to seeing that relevant matters were taken into account and irrelevant matters excluded. Apart from that it will not interfere unless the decision is shown to be so unreasonable that no reasonable body could have made it. But that does not mean that the Court must agree with the local authority's decision. It may disagree with it strongly yet hold it to be reasonable. The Court is in no sense an appellate authority reviewing the decisions of the licensing body, but is concerned only to see that they have not exceeded their powers.[1]

A similar doctrine has been enunciated with even greater

[1]*Associated Provincial Picture Houses Ltd. v. Wednesbury Corporation* (1948) 1 K.B., at pp. 230-1, 233-4.

force in regard to town and country planning. The Court of Appeal has said that "Parliament meant these matters to be left to the decision of the elected local authority. It is for them to consider, and not for a Court, what it is desirable should be done or not done in relation to these schemes; and, provided that they are acting *intra vires*, their action cannot be controlled by the Courts."[1] In making a compulsory purchase order to enable land in a war-damaged area to be laid out afresh and redeveloped as a whole the Minister of Town and Country Planning is to be sole judge. He is acting in an executive capacity and may arrive at his decision on whatever grounds he thinks fit. Moreover, he cannot be compelled to disclose to the Court the material which has come to him in performing this function, for that would be detrimental to the public interest.[2] In the Stevenage case[3] the House of Lords affirmed the decision of the Court of Appeal that the Minister of Town and Country Planning is not acting judicially in making an order under the New Towns Act. Hence it is irrelevant to allege bias on the Minister's part so long as he conforms with the procedure laid down by the statute, In this case the House of Lords rejected an attempt to judicialise administration, which, if it had succeeded, would have made it almost impossible for the Minister to take effective action under the New Towns Act.

In the long line of housing cases which were decided in the 1930's,[4] objectors to compulsory purchase or clearance orders usually alleged that the Minister of Health in confirming the order, or the local authority in making it, had infringed the rules of natural justice. The decision frequently depended on whether the Court regarded the particular stage of the proceedings to which objection was taken, as judicial or quasi-judicial in character: or, conversely, as ministerial or admini-

[1] *Taylor v. Brighton Borough Council* (1947) K.B. 736, at p. 742; *Swindon Corporation v. Pearce and another*, 64 T.L.R., p. 323.
[2] *Robinson and others v. Minister of Town and Country Planning* (1947) 63 T.L.R., pp. 374, 377.
[3] *Franklin and others v. Minister of Town and Country Planning* (1947) 63 T.L.R., p. 446.
[4] *Errington v. Minister of Health* (1935) 1 K.B., 249; *Frost v. Minister of Health* (1935) 1 K.B. 286; *Offer v. Minister of Health* (1936) 1 K.B. 40; *Horn v. Minister of Health* (1937) 1 K.B. 626.

strative.[1] Thus, in Errington's case[2] it was said that when the Minister deals with a clearance order under the Housing Act, 1930 to which no objection has been taken he is acting administratively; but that when an objection has been lodged he is exercising a quasi-judicial function. There is little distinction in the Minister's function at either stage. But the practical importance of the Court's finding is that the rules of natural justice apply when the Minister is acting judicially but not when he is engaged in administration.[3]

It follows that when the Courts conceive executive discretion in narrow terms, they will tend to enlarge the area of the administrative process comprised within the judicial or "quasi-judicial" category; while when their attitude towards the executive is more indulgent they will be disposed to hold that specified activities are administrative in character. There are, of course, limits to the extent to which the frontier between judicial and administrative functions can be moved in either direction by judicial decision; but anyone who is acquainted with the cases will agree that there is a considerable area within which movement can and does take place.

This is illustrated by two recent cases. In *Stafford v. Minister of Health*[4] a landowner had given notice of objection on several grounds to a compulsory purchase order for housing purposes. Under the Housing (Temporary Provisions) Act, 1944, the Minister was not obliged to hold a local enquiry and he did not order one in this instance. Unknown to the plaintiff, he forwarded the notice of objection to the local authority, which then sent detailed replies to the grounds of objection. This statement was not transmitted to Stafford and he had no opportunity of answering the contentions which it contained. Charles, J., held that the Minister, who was acting in a judicial capacity, had not given the objector a fair opportunity for putting his case, thereby contravening the principles of British justice. In *Miller v. Minister of Health*,[5] the Minister informed the plaintiff that his

---

[1] I do not agree with this terminology. It is, however, in general use in the Courts and I reproduce it for that reason.

[2] *Errington v. Minister of Health* (1934) 51 T.L.R., p. 44.

[3] See the comment in Annual Survey of English Law, 1934, p. 33.

[4] [1946] 1 K.B. 621; 62 T.L.R., p. 451.   [5] [1946] 1 K.B. 626; 62 T.L.R., p. 611.

notice of objection had not been submitted to the local authority but that the department had sufficient information in its possession to be able to consider the objections without obtaining the views of the Council or hearing any elaboration of the objections. The information which the department possessed was not disclosed to the objector. He therefore complained that he had not been informed of the reasons why the local authority supported the plan, nor had an opportunity to comment on those reasons or to amplify his notice of objection. The Court held that the Minister had acted administratively in acquiring the information some months prior to receiving notice of objection. There was no substantial complaint which could be made against the Minister for considering this information before he was asked to act in a judicial capacity. Moreover, the plaintiff had no right to amplify his grounds of objection, since there was nothing to show that the Minister had not accepted all his contentions yet nevertheless decided to confirm the order on administrative grounds. Since there are no limitations imposed by natural justice on administrative action, the Minister's failure to allow Mr. Miller to elaborate his objections could not be held to be contrary to natural justice.

The distinction between these cases is so nebulous as to be almost non-existent, so far as any clear principle is concerned. The element of uncertainty is very large in the sphere of natural justice; but whereas one could detect a tendency in the 1930's to enlarge the scope of its application, since 1945 the tendency seems to have been in the opposite direction. This contraction conforms to the recent trend of the Courts towards self-limitation in matters of public administration.

We must, however, be careful not to oversimplify or exaggerate the situation. During and since the war of 1939-45 the Courts have been more willing than formerly to recognise the great powers conferred on the executive and to regard public authorities as responsible bodies who may properly be entrusted with large discretions which are not liable to judicial review unless illegality is clearly shown. Thus in *Progressive Supply Co.*

Ltd. v. Dalton,[1] Mr. Justice Farwell said that if the Crown makes defence regulations and orders, the necessity for them must be assumed and the Court would not hear evidence on that point. Nonetheless, the judges remain zealous to see that both central and local authorities keep within their statutory powers and also follow strictly any prescribed procedure. In 1936, the King's Bench prohibited the Minister of Health from allowing the London County Council to appropriate part of Hackney Marshes for housing purposes, on the ground that it would contravene the provisions of the London Open Spaces Act 1893.[2] More recently, a War Agricultural Executive Committee, to which the Minister of Agriculture and Fisheries had delegated his powers relating to the cultivation and use of land under the defence regulations, ordered a farmer to grow 8 acres of sugar beet but left it to their executive officer to designate the precise area on which the beet was to be grown. In due course the officer served a notice on behalf of the Executive Committee directing the beet to be grown in a specified field. On appeal the Court held that the Executive Committee had no power to delegate to its executive officer the selection of the land to be cultivated. The notices were in consequence invalid.[3] The maxim *delegatus non potest delegare* is an old one; but this case illustrates the insistence of the Courts that administration should take place within the procedural framework prescribed by law.

I now turn to the legal liabilities of public authorities for wrongful acts. The outstanding event of the period under review was the passing of the Crown Proceedings Act, 1947. The abolition of the immunity of the Crown in tort would alone suffice to make this statute of great historic importance. But it does far more than that. It abolishes the petition of right, a cumbersome procedure which required the fiat of the Attorney-General, and enables the subject to pursue contractual claims as of right. It makes departments responsible to their employees for any breach of statutory duties, such as a failure to observe

[1] (1943) 1 Ch. p. 55.
[2] *R. v. Minister of Health, ex parte Villiers* (1936) 2 K.B., p. 29.
[3] *Allingham and Another v. Ministry of Agriculture & Fisheries*, 64 T.L.R., p. 290,

the requirements of the Factories Act; and also for the duties which at common law an employer owes his servants or agents. It imposes on the Crown all the common law duties attaching to the ownership, occupation, possession or control of property. It sweeps away all the archaic procedures used in Crown proceedings such as Latin information, English information, writs of *scire facias* and other relics of the past and to a large extent assimilates proceedings by or against the Crown to those between private persons. It applies (with slight exceptions) the law of civil salvage, whether of life or property, to salvage services rendered to His Majesty's ships or aircraft, or in saving life or cargo therefrom. It enables civil proceedings against the Crown to be instituted in the County Court. There are exceptions, savings and provisos in the Act which preserve certain privileges of the Crown. The postal services and the armed forces (internally) have preserved and even increased their immunity from legal action; but in substance the statute makes the State for the first time legally responsible for its actions.

So great a reform could only be accomplished by legislation. All branches of the legal profession, and men of all political opinions, had for more than twenty years clamoured for it. In order to avoid the injustice resulting from Crown immunity for civil wrongs a practice had grown up whereby Government departments allowed an action to proceed against a named person who was really representing the department. His name would be supplied on request; and if judgment were given against him the department paid the damages and costs.[1] This legal fiction worked fairly well until it was exploded by the House of Lords in *Adams v. Naylor*.[2] In that case Lord Simon rejected the suggestion that Captain Naylor could be referred to as the "nominal" or "nominated" defendant. "Such language," he said, "seems to suggest that the issues at the trial are really issues between the plaintiffs and the Crown and that the defendant is mentioned as a party merely as a matter of convenience. That is not the true position. The Courts before

[1] *Royster v. Cavey* (1947), 1 K.B., p. 204; Scott L. J., at pp. 206-7.
[2] (1946) A.C., p. 543.

143

whom such a case as this comes have to decide it as between the parties before them and have nothing to do with the fact that the Crown stands behind the defendant."[1] The plaintiffs cannot succeed without showing that the defendant himself owed a duty of care to them which he failed to discharge. This statement was *obiter*, since it was in no way necessary to the decision, which was given on other grounds; but it sufficed to induce the Court of Appeal subsequently to reject an appeal from a County Court decision in *Royster v. Cavey*.[2] In this action the plaintiff was an employee of a Royal Ordnance factory occupied by the Ministry of Supply. She fell into a trench across the road along which she had to walk and sued the Superintendent of the Royal Ordnance factory at Maltby for negligence or breach of statutory duty. He had nothing to do with the accident; he was not the occupier of the factory; he had not been guilty of any negligence or breach of statutory duty. He had been named by the Treasury Solicitor as the proper person to sue; and the Treasury Solicitor expressly disclaimed any wish to rely on the defendant's lack of personal responsibility for what had occurred. But the Court of Appeal would not heed this generous gesture, the beneficent bluff was called and in exposing it Lord Justice Scott solemnly declared that it would be "a crying wrong if that legislation [the Crown Proceedings Bill] is not introduced at an early date."[3] The Bill was introduced shortly afterwards and received widespread acclamation.

There are several other statutes which have reformed the law concerning judicial control of administration. The Administration of Justice (Miscellaneous Provisions) Act, 1938, abolished the ancient prerogative writs of mandamus, certiorari, prohibition, etc., and substituted in their place orders of like effect. These orders can be sought or obtained by a simpler procedure. The Limitation Act, 1939 increased from six months to a year the time limit within which actions must be brought against public authorities. In numerous spheres of administration statutory remedies have replaced common law remedies.

[1]*Ibid.*, at p. 550.
[2](1947) I K.B., p. 204.
[3] *Ibid.*, at p. 210.

144

Most actions in tort against public authorities are based on allegations of negligence or nuisance. We may divide them into three main classes for the purpose of this brief review. There are those which relate to injuries caused by the highway; those where patients in hospital have been treated negligently; and the more general cases illustrating the legal liability of public authorities towards members of the public.

The general rule that a local authority is liable for the negligence of its servants in the same way as an ordinary person[1] is subject to the exception that a highway authority is not liable for injuries caused by non-feasance, i.e. failure to repair or maintain the road. There is no logic or sense in this exception nowadays: it originated in the procedural difficulty of suing the inhabitants of an unincorporated county in the 18th century, when there was no representative body that could be made liable.[2] The exception has been affirmed in a line of cases extending to our own day.[3] In recent years, however, the Courts have avoided the rule whenever it appeared possible to devise and apply ingenious reasoning for that purpose.

Thus, in *Guilfoyle v. Port of London Authority*,[4] the plaintiff had been injured by falling over a projecting nail on a swing bridge which connected two highways serving the London docks. The Port of London Authority, which had a statutory duty to repair the bridge, had negligently failed to carry out their obligation. They contended that they had been guilty only of non-feasance in respect of a highway. The Court held that the bridge was not a highway and that the defendants were therefore liable.

In *Skilton v. Epsom and Ewell Urban District Council*[5] a passing motor car caused a traffic stud in the highway to fly up and strike a bicycle, making it overturn. The injured cyclist sued the local authority, which had placed the studs in position under powers conferred by the Road Traffic Act, 1930. They pleaded non-feasance. The Court held that the defendants could not

[1] *Mersey Docks & Harbour Board v. Gibbs* (1866) L.R. 1 H.L. 93.
[2] *Russell v. Men of Devon* (1788) 2 T.R. 667.
[3] *Cowley v. Newmarket Local Board* (1892) A.C., p. 345.
[4] (1932) 1 K.B., p. 336.
[5] (1937) 1 K.B., p. 112. See also *Newsome v. Darton U.D.C.* 54 T.L.R., p. 286, where the local authority was acting as the sanitary authority when it disturbed the road.

take advantage of the cases dealing with maintenance of highways, because the stud was not placed by them on the highway in the performance of their road maintenance functions under the Highways Act, 1835, but for the purpose of traffic direction under the Road Traffic Act, 1930.

In another case[1] a boy cyclist met with a fatal accident owing to the failure of a metropolitan borough council to remove the track of an abandoned tramway and to restore the surface of the road to its former condition. The local authority had notified their intention of carrying out the work under an option given to them by the London Passenger Transport Act, 1933. They pleaded non-feasance but the Court rejected the defence. The immunity conferred on a highway authority by the non-feasance rule is limited to those duties which fall on a local highway authority acting in that capacity.

The status of a highway authority is to be strictly construed. Where the Minister of Transport delegated his functions relating to certain trunk roads to a county council, including the provision and maintenance of fences necessary for the support or protection of the highway, it was held that the Minister was the real and only highway authority and the county council were mere contractors. Hence, they were not a public authority performing an act in the direct execution of a statute or in the discharge of a public duty. "They do not become highway authority because they act under a contract with a highway authority." In consequence they were liable to the widow of a man who lost his life through an accident resulting from the absence of a proper fence needed to guard a footpath which ended in a drop on to the main road. The judge found the county council had committed misfeasance; but even if it had been non-feasance they could not have escaped liability as they were not the highway authority.[2]

This accident, like many others which occurred during the war of 1939-45, was caused partly by the black-out. The numerous injuries caused by collisions between motor vehicles, cyclists or pedestrians and unlighted air-raid shelters, led the

[1] *Simon v. Islington Borough Council,* 59 T.L.R., p. 87.
[2] *Drake v. Bedfordshire County Council,* 60 T.L.R., p. 304.

Courts to reconsider carefully the nature of the duties falling on highway authorities which had provided these shelters. After numerous conflicting decisions the law was clarified in *Fisher v. Ruislip-Northwood Urban District Council and Middlesex County Council*.[1] The plaintiff was driving a motor-car at night when he ran into an air-raid surface shelter erected in the roadway. Street lighting was prohibited at the time, but the shelter was fitted with danger lights which were unlighted at the time of the accident. The judge of first instance held there was no duty to light the shelter. On appeal, the Master of the Rolls reviewed the long line of cases bearing on this subject. He explained that legislation authorising public work does not usually impose a duty on the undertakers to exercise care in construction and maintenance; but it is well established that they are not entitled in law to disregard the safety of other persons. The extent of the duty varies with the circumstances; and in an extreme case, if it were impossible by any precautions to render the works safe, it might well be that no liability would fall on the authority for undertaking them. The obligation of the authority is, however, to take reasonable precautions to safeguard the public from danger, both by day and by night. This must be conceived in general terms and not as an obligation limited to lighting the highway or an obstruction on it. Here the duty had not been discharged and the plaintiff therefore succeeded in his action.

The hospital cases are of increasing interest since the inception of the national health service, for now anyone may become a patient in a State hospital. The legal obligations of hospital authorities are therefore of general significance. The earlier decisions established that a hospital authority which takes care to appoint properly qualified physicians and surgeons, and to provide proper equipment and premises for them, will not be liable for their negligence in medical matters.[2] A consulting physician or surgeon in exercising his skill is an independent professional practitioner not subject to instruction about his work. Hence the relationship of master and servant

[1] (1945) 1 K.B., p. 584.
[2] *Hillyer v. St. Bartholomew's Hospital*, L.J. 1909 N.S. 78 K.B.D., p. 958; *Evans v. Liverpool Corporation* (1906) 1 K.B., p. 160.

does not subsist between him and the hospital authority for the purpose of making the latter vicariously liable for his wrongdoing.

This left unmapped a very large area of hospital management and medical treatment. Some of the recent cases have helped to chart it. In *Gold v. Essex County Council*[1] the visiting dermatologist at a county hospital prescribed facial treatment by Grenz rays for the plaintiff. This was given by a competent and properly qualified radiographer who on one occasion negligently failed to screen the patient's face with the correct material, with the result that she suffered injury. The trial judge decided for the defendants on the ground that they employed a competent and skilled radiographer and were not responsible for his negligence in a professional matter. The Court of Appeal reversed this decision and raised the standard of liability much higher. The Public Health Act, 1936 imposes an obligation on local authorities, if they exercise the powers conferred on them to treat patients. It follows that the authority will be liable if those whom they employ under a contract of service to perform that obligation act negligently. The county council's duty includes the provision of nursing; and if the nurses are negligent the council is liable. A nurse who carries out with due care the instruction of a surgeon or doctor cannot be held negligent, however negligent the instructions may be; and therefore the hospital authority is not liable for the results of her action in such circumstances. Here, however, the radiographer was acting on his own responsibility and according to his own judgment. The only orders he obeyed were as to the nature and amount of treatment he was to give. The county council were therefore liable as hospital authority for his negligence.

In *Marshall v. Lindsey County Council*[2] the question in issue was whether the local authority was liable in damages to the plaintiff, who had contracted puerperal fever in consequence of being confined in a maternity home provided by them. An outbreak of puerperal fever had occurred at the home shortly before Mrs. Marshall was admitted but neither she nor her own

[1] 58 T.L.R., p. 357; L.R. (1942) 2 K.B. 293.
[2] (1935) 1 K.B. 516; (1937) A.C. 97.

doctor (who was attending her) were notified. The jury found the defendant council had been negligent in admitting new patients after the outbreak first occurred, in not informing the plaintiff or her doctor, and in not taking swabs from every member of the staff. Judgment was given for the plaintiff. The decision was upheld by the Court of Appeal and by the House of Lords. Lord Hailsham, the Lord Chancellor, rejected the plea that the defendants were entitled to rely on their medical advisers. They had a duty laid upon them by law and they were responsible for the mistakes of their agents. There is, he said, no difference in principle between the employment of a doctor to advise on medical questions and the employment of any other skilled person to advise upon other questions.[1] Although the plaintiff was not receiving medical treatment from physicians or surgeons on the staff of the maternity home, it is a far cry from this decision to Hillyer's case.

The most recent case was *Collins v. Hertfordshire County Council and Another.*[2] This action arose through H., a visiting surgeon, giving instructions by telephone to Miss K., a medical student acting as resident junior house surgeon, about an operation which he was to perform next day on C., the plaintiff's husband. H. ordered "procaine" in the anaesthetic; Miss K. understood him to say "cocaine." The pharmacist dispensed the solution on Miss K.'s verbal instruction, which should have been in writing, and did not place it in a coloured "poison" bottle with fluted sides. The solution was lethal and the patient died immediately it was injected. Hilbery, J. found that the hospital had permitted a dangerous and negligent system to be operated in the provision of dangerous drugs. In the result, the county council were held liable as hospital authority for the negligence of the resident junior house surgeon but not for that of the visiting surgeon, who was personally liable as joint tortfeasor.

The decision in *Martin v. London County Council*[3] relates to the responsibility of hospital authorities for property belonging to their patients. The plaintiff was brought to a mental hospital by

[1]*Ibid.*, at pp. 106, 108.
[2](1947) 1 K.B. 599.
[3](1947) 1 K.B. 628.

the relieving officer and a reception order was made for her under the Lunacy Act, 1890. Her estate became liable to defray the cost of her maintenance. She had with her in her handbag two valuable pieces of jewellery and a gold cigarette case. These articles were taken from her in accordance with the usual routine of the hospital, and stored in an unsafe place from which they were subsequently stolen by a thief. The Official Solicitor recovered damages on her behalf from the managers of the hospital, who had failed to exercise the standard of care required of bailees for reward.

A point about this decision which the layman may not appreciate is that the hospital authority were required to observe a higher standard of care in safeguarding the property of this patient than if she had not been a paying patient. In the latter event they would have been in the position of gratuitous bailees and liable only for gross negligence.[1]

This tendency to diminish the degree of liability imposed on public authorities towards those who use the services provided for the general public and which are paid for out of taxation, rather than by a special charge levied on the individual, is one of the chief defects in the legal remedies available against the executive.

This defect is visible in some of the cases concerning the general liabilities of local authorities in tort, to which I will now turn.

One would expect that a very high standard of care would be exacted of local authorities in dealing with children; but this is far from being the attitude of the Courts. In *Ellis v. Fulham Borough Council*[2] the plaintiff was a small boy who had paddled in a paddling pool provided by the defendant council. In so doing so he had cut his foot on a piece of glass embedded in the sand. The local authority was aware of the danger to children from sharp materials or implements getting buried in the sand; but their arrangements for raking the pool were inadequate. The trial judge held that the plaintiff was an invitee and decided in his favour. The Court of Appeal affirmed the decision but—

---

[1] *Ibid.* Henn Collins, J. at p. 630.
[2] (1937) 1 K.B., p. 212.

and it is an important qualification—they treated the plaintiff as a licensee. The standard of care due to a licensee is much lower than that owed to an invitee, since it extends only to hidden dangers known to the authority but not to the licensee and which the latter can not be expected to avoid. In Ellis's case there was such a danger so the result was not affected. But in *Sutton v. Bootle Corporation*[1] a finding that the plaintiff, a little girl of 9, was only a licensee when using a children's playground in a municipal recreation ground, defeated her claim for loss of a finger which was crushed in a checking device on a plank-swing. As licensors the Corporation were under no greater duty than to warn or protect children of dangers actually known to them. As they had no knowledge of any danger arising from this type of swing they had committed no breach of duty. The judge of first instance had held that a local authority which provides equipment for children in a public recreation ground has a duty to provide safe and proper implements so far as care and skill can make them so, and he gave for the plaintiff. The Court of Appeal reversed his decision because it laid upon the Corporation a measure of duty erroneous in law.

A very bad example of the inability of the Courts to discern and formulate a satisfactory relationship between the public authority and a citizen was *Travers v. Gloucester Corporation and Another.*[2] This action arose from the death of Richard Travers, who was asphyxiated in his bath by poisonous fumes emitted by a geyser. The gas had been turned off at the time of his death. The house where the accident occurred was a council house in which he was lodging. It was one of a large number built for the Gloucester Corporation by a firm of contractors. The contract provided that geysers should be fitted in accordance with the directions of the borough architect. The method of installing geysers in the house in question and others of similar type was dangerous and unsatisfactory. The local gas company had in the preceding year written to the local authority drawing their attention to the defective fitting and had pointed out that alteration was necessary. Alterations were carried out in some

[1] (1947) 1 K.B., p. 359.
[2] (1946) 62 T.L.R., p. 723.

houses on the estate, but not in the one where the fatality occurred. At the trial the Corporation contended that they owed no duty to the deceased man; or, alternatively, that if they did they had not committed any breach of duty. Mr. Justice Lewis concluded with some regret that the case must be dealt with according to the principles governing the rights and duties of landlords and tenants. This meant applying Sir William Erle's dictum in 1863 that "A landlord who lets a house in a dangerous state, is not liable to the tenant's customers or guests for accidents happening during the term; for, fraud apart, there is no law against letting a tumble-down house, and the tenant's remedy is upon his contract, if any."[1]

To assimilate the position of a local housing authority to that of a private landlord is to apply an entirely false analogy and also to ignore the spirit and intent of the housing legislation of the past 50 years; to deny that a local housing authority has any duty towards members of the public other than its tenants for dangers and defects in council houses is to misconceive the nature of local government and of the municipal housing movement; to limit the rights of the tenant to those arising from his contract is even more archaic where the landlord is a local authority than where the house is in private ownership.

A more liberal and modern outlook is to be found in the judgment in the Croydon water case.[2] The plaintiffs were a ratepayer and his infant daughter who had contracted typhoid fever through drinking contaminated water supplied by the county borough council. Stable, J. held that the Corporation was guilty of a breach of statutory duty under the Waterworks Clauses Act towards Mr. Read in his capacity as ratepayer. They owed no statutory duty to his daughter. There was, however, a duty at common law to take reasonable care, and this was owed to all members of the public. The Corporation had contended that the provision of a remedy in the water legislation for a breach of the statutory duty excluded any other remedy arising at common law or otherwise, but the learned

[1]*Robbins v. Jones* (1863) 15 C.B. (N.S.) at p. 240. See also *Bottomley v. Bannister* (1932) 1 K.B. 458.
[2]*Read v. Croydon Corporation* (1938) 4 All.E.R., p. 631.

judge rejected this argument. "It would indeed," he said, "be an extraordinary result if Miss Read were to be deprived of her remedy at common law because of the existence of an Act of Parliament which imposes a duty, but not a duty to her, and which sets up a remedy for breach of that duty of which she can never be in a position to take advantage".[1] In considering whether the existence of statutory penalty excludes any other right of action, Mr. Justice Stable said the criterion is to be found in the intention of the Act, with particular reference to whether a duty is owed primarily to the state or community and only incidentally to the individual, or primarily to the individual or class of individuals, and only incidentally to the state or community.[2] Applying that criterion to the Waterworks Clauses Acts, he found that while for breaches of some duties the statutory penalties are exclusive, for others they would not be.[3] In the result both plaintiffs succeeded.

In this case, as in all other actions for negligence, the Court had to decide whether the public authority has shown a "reasonable" degree of care or "due skill" in devising safeguards against dangers arising from the services it provides. Neither under statute nor at common law do public authorities appear to be liable for damage resulting from their activities irrespective of negligence, nuisance, or some other form of moral culpability. Whether this qualified standard suffices to afford adequate protection to the public against inherent dangers or defects in public services is doubtful. It proved totally insufficient in the sphere of industrial injuries, where the common law liabilities of employers, founded on the notion of moral culpability, were replaced by the doctrine of absolute risk embodied in the Workmen's Compensation Acts and more recently in the new social insurance scheme for industrial injuries. The doctrine of absolute risk means that a public authority can be held liable for injuries to person or property from causes inherent in the functions it performs, irrespective of any fault or neglect. It is already firmly rooted in the juris-

[1] *Ibid.*, at p. 650.
[2] *Ibid.*, p. 652.
[3] *Manchester Corporation v. Farnworth* (1930) A.C. 171.

153

prudence of the *Conseil d'Etat*. It has so far gained no footing in English public law except in war-time legislation such as the Personal Injuries (Emergency Powers) Act, 1939.

This brief review of judicial control of public administration during the last 25 years shows that although some of the long established principles of tortious liability have sufficed to meet modern needs, there has been a total absence of creative innovation in the Courts. The great milestone of the period is the work of Parliament—the Crown Proceedings Act.

The law of negligence and nuisance is valuable if—and only if—the standard of care owed to the public is set sufficiently high. The hospital cases offer the most hopeful example in this respect. Where, however, children or adult citizens using public services are relegated to the category of mere licensees, the relationship is full of potential injustice, whatever the result may be on the facts of particular cases. The application of private law rules of liability to the obligations of a local housing authority, and the consequent denial of any right other than that arising from contract, is fundamentally wrong.

The principles of natural justice have proved increasingly unsubstantial as a method of controlling administration. Even where they apply to executive authorities acting in a judicial capacity, they touch only the form and method of the proceedings rather than the substance of the decision. It is improbable that any significant development of these principles will take place.

The greatest weakness of judicial control is the inability of the Courts to compel public authorities to carry out their positive duties or to provide an adequate remedy for failure to do so. The judges are clearly unwilling to extend the immunity of highway authorities for non-feasance and seem anxious to restrict its operation as narrowly as possible. But what remedy does the law afford to the child whose future is jeopardised by the failure of the local education authority to provide proper schools; to the slum dwellers who cannot obtain better housing conditions owing to the failure of the local authority to perform their duties; to the business man whose premises are destroyed by fire owing to the defective equipment or operation of the

154

local fire brigade; to the householders who suffer frequent incon-
venience and hardship owing to failure of gas or electricity
supplies? The answer is that no legal remedy is available in
most instances either in the form of damages or of compulsory
enforcement of duty. An order of mandamus is seldom sought
and seldom granted. It is, indeed, inappropriate to circumstances such as these, in view of the precedents which narrowly
confine its use.

Many people are disposed to think that it is not the function
of a Court to provide remedies, or to exercise a preventive
jurisdiction, for failure of public authorities to perform their
functions. That, they say, is a task for Parliament, which
can bring pressure to bear on the Government or pass new
legislation; or, where a local authority is recalcitrant, the
Minister in charge of the appropriate department should intervene or alternatively the voters can elect a different council at
the next election. This lack of confidence in judicial control and
the attendant belief in political control may well reflect the
prevailing mood. It leads inevitably to a diminution in the
scope and importance of the rôle of the Courts in relation to
public administration. This is precisely the trend which has
occurred during the past 25 years. Judicial control has been on
the wane.

In my opinion this is an unhealthy state of affairs. It is bad for
the Executive and detrimental to the Rule of Law, on any
reasonable interpretation of that much-abused expression. It is,
however, likely to continue until such time as we recognise the
need to set up an Administrative Court or Courts. Only by that
means can we hope to obtain the freshness of view, release from
a mass of binding precedents unsuited to modern conditions,
the sloughing off of private law doctrines, the concentration of
attention on the problems peculiar to the Administrative State,
the adoption of more liberal canons of statutory interpretation,
and other changes of method which are necessary if a great
creative effort is to be made in this branch of administrative law.

The attitude both of lawyers and of laymen towards Administrative Law is much more rational and tolerant than formerly.
Lawyers and politicians no longer deny that we have a vast

body of Administrative Law in England. No one any longer becomes indignant at the mere suggestion, as though it were a slur on the fair name of Britain. Future progress will depend very largely on the quality and quantity of public law teaching and research in the Universities and the professional law schools, and whether Parliament takes a serious and continuing interest in the subject.

QUASI-GOVERNMENT BODIES
SINCE 1918

by Sir Arthur Street, G.C.B., K.B.E., C.M.G., C.I.E., M.C.

1. Introduction

"What's a quasi-Government body?" asked Alice. "It's the devil," shrieked the Red Queen, "it's bourgeois and worse it's State capitalism." "It's the devil," wailed the walrus, "it kills enterprise," while the jabbercolquahock, fast asleep, murmured between snores, "Civil Service, red-tape, bureaucracy." "But," began Alice, "how can it mean all these things at the same time?" "It does," I said, "it's the devil all right. It can mean all things to all men. It's not going to mean local authorities because they are being dealt with in another Chapter nor, for the same reason, is it going to mean administrative tribunals, nor is it going to mean Royal Commissions and bodies set up to advise the Government on this or that, for no better reason than that there is no room to deal with them. The great thing nowadays is to make words mean what you want them to mean. It does not matter if no-one else knows what you are talking about. It's like decentralisation, proletarianisation, de-functionalisation, departmentalisation, or the distinction between policy and execution." With the mention of the word "execution," there was a sullen growl from the multitude. "I ought to know," I said, "I am associated with a quasi-Government body." At this, brick-bats started flying in all directions and I retreated to an atomic bomb-proof shelter, the nearest and deepest, to review the subject with philosophic detachment.

Quasi-Government bodies are no new thing in our history. For centuries Government had concerned itself mainly with law and order, defence, external relations and the collection of taxes. Gradually it extended its field and the first steps were usually hesitant—a commission to supervise this, a committee to deal with that. With the growth of the doctrine of Ministerial responsibility in the last 100 years, most of these commissions and committees came home to roost in some Government Department.

When the "Three Kings of Somerset House," the Poor Law Commissioners, set up in 1834, had come to grief in a furious storm of controversy, a Poor Law Board with a Minister at its head had to be substituted; this and similar experiences had taught the lesson that ventilation of grievances by representatives of the people and defence in Parliament by a responsible Member of the Government were essential, not only to the vitality of democracy but also to the efficiency of administration. Thus in 1918, when the period we are reviewing started, quasi-Government bodies came up for judgment by the Haldane Committee and received sentence of death. The Committee said:—

"In some cases recourse has been had to the system of administrative Boards. We draw attention to the finding of the Royal Commission on the Civil Service (Cmd. 7338) that this system is less effective in securing responsibility for official action and advice than the system followed in Departments where full responsibility is definitely laid upon the Minister; and we think that where, as in the case of the Insurance Commissioners, a Board is set up without explicit statutory provision for a Minister responsible to Parliament for their work the position is obviously unsatisfactory.... We are so far from thinking that the importance of a service to the community is prima facie a reason for making those who administer it immune from ordinary Parliamentary criticism that we feel that all such proposals should be most carefully scrutinised and that there should be no omission, in the case of any particular service, of those safeguards which Ministerial responsibility to Parliament alone provides."[1]

The next year, some quasi-Government bodies did, in fact, disappear. One, the Road Board, set up by Mr. Lloyd George's Development and Road Improvement Funds Act of 1909, was supplanted by the Ministry of Transport. The Board had had power, with Treasury approval, to make advances to Highway Authorities for road construction or improvement and also

[1]Cmd. 9230/1918, page 11.

itself to construct and maintain new roads. Similarly, the Insurance Commissions (for England, Scotland, Wales and Ireland), set up by the National Insurance Act 1911 for the central administration of National Health Insurance, were abolished on the transfer of their powers to the newly-created Health Departments in 1919. Other bodies had suffered a like fate in the past (e.g. the Land Commissioners absorbed in the Board of Agriculture on its formation in 1889). These bodies were a sort of patrolling force over ground which was destined to be fully occupied by a regular Government Department.

Generally speaking, however, the sentence of the Haldane Committee was not carried out. It was perhaps not intended to touch bodies like professional institutions empowered by statute to regulate the affairs of their professions, and public utilities like the Port of London Authority and the Metropolitan Water Board. Nor was it heeded in the decades which followed, when there was a proliferation of quasi-Government bodies of all kinds—boards, authorities, commissions, councils, committees, corporations and executives. The reasons are not far to seek. For many years now, the activities of Government have been spreading until they touch almost every aspect of the economic and social life of the community. It was necessary for Government to delegate responsibility to quasi-Government bodies to relieve the growing burden on Ministers and their Civil Service advisers, to enlist special skills and experience and to enable large enterprises to operate as businesses on behalf of the State untrammelled by the checks and controls inseparable from day-to-day accountability of a Minister to Parliament.

Changes in the functions of Government have had their counterpart in changed relationships between Government and governed. In Gladstone's day, it was primarily as a tax-payer that the average voter was interested in the doings of the State. Now he is also interested as a consumer of coal, as a user of transport, as a listener to the wireless, as a viewer of television and as a patient of the National Health Service. If he is an employee of one of the nationalised industries, he will probably have a lively interest in the functions of the State as an employer. In this new democracy, the electorate will no doubt demand that Parliamentary control over the agents of executive Government shall be effective, but they are likely to demand also that it shall be exercised in such a way as not to hamper the efficiency of the enterprises which serve their daily lives.

The 19th century's constitutional lesson of Ministerial responsibility has not been forgotten, but it has had to be adapted to fit new circumstances. Although the Acts of Parliament setting up quasi-Governmental bodies have imposed all varieties and degrees of Ministerial control, the constitutional practice has gradually crystallised out. The Minister appoints the members of the body and leaves them in post only for so long as he considers them to be efficiently carrying out their functions. He has the power to issue directions on general matters affecting the national interest and is responsible to Parliament for the way he exercises or fails to exercise that power. The body itself must present an annual report and audited accounts to the Minister, who in turn lays them before Parliament. Parliament thus has an opportunity from time to time of discussing the affairs of the body in a general way. The Minister, however, does not answer Questions in Parliament about day-to-day details of management or administration for which not he but the body is responsible either explicitly or implicitly under the statute which set it up. The Minister may retain responsibility and have powers in one or two special fields, e.g. to approve borrowing which may pledge the Government's credit, to approve estimates of expenditure where they have to be defrayed out of monies voted by Parliament, to protect the health and safety of employees or to see that equitable superannuation schemes are established. The extent of his special responsibilities depends on the circumstances of each quasi-Government body and he is fully answerable to Parliament for his discharge of them.

It is, however, unsafe to generalise about quasi-Government bodies. Like flowers in Spring, they have grown as variously and profusely and with as little regard for conventional patterns. They are even less susceptible of orderly classification: with quasi-Government bodies, a new species often suggests a new genus. For convenience, they will here be discussed under the headings of Regulatory Bodies (Non-Industrial), Regulatory Bodies (Industrial) and Managerial Bodies, but the classification is imperfect and artificial.

The first of these headings covers quasi-Government bodies used, to adapt Clausewitz, for Departmental administration carried on by other means. Under the second are bodies largely concerned with relationships between Government and private industry; if they stem from Government, they have thrown out roots into commercial and industrial soil. In the third group are the managerial bodies, including the large State industrial and trading corporations which are themselves a part of industry and commerce; in many ways, they are the logical development, constitutionally if not politically, of the other groups; they have great opportunities and hence great responsibilities for organising the production and distribution of goods so as best to serve the national economy; the importance of their economic function is one of their characteristics; others are their intimate concern with labour relations, the technique of management and the problems of size.

The three groups have one thing in common. They are all projections of Government and they have a clear purpose which they share with Government Departments, the Armed Forces and Local Authorities, to serve the public to the best of their endeavours. While no-one would claim that the employees of quasi-Government bodies should live as ascetically as monks or as impecuniously as Plato's guardians or that personal ambition, within legitimate bounds, should not spur them to greater effort, yet the mainspring of action should not be hope of gain alone. There is a more profound source of inspiration, call it esprit de corps or patriotism or the ideal of public service or more simply the desire to live a useful and not merely selfish life. In time of war or national danger, it has often released vast reserves of hidden energy. So now, day by day, it should shape the traditions and codes of conduct of the new public services as of the old, and powerfully reinforce the purely material incentives towards the full realisation of the individual and the good of the community as a whole.

2. REGULATORY BODIES (NON-INDUSTRIAL)

While since 1918 the quasi-Government body has been used more and more as an instrument of State for the assistance, control or management of industries, it has continued to have older uses, such as the discharge of technical and specialist functions which, in spite of and often because of their discretionary character, are not considered appropriate for a Government Department.

In the line of development from the Ecclesiastical Commission (now called the Church Commissioners) and the Charity Commission, set up in the 19th century, and from the Crown Lands Commission, which under previous titles has a long history going back over several centuries, is for example the Tithe Redemption Commission created by the Tithe Act of 1936. The Commission's duties involve a great deal of detailed and technical work; among other things they have to determine how much stock to issue and to whom in compensation for extinguished rent charges and to fix and collect the redemption annuities. The Commission is appointed by the Treasury after consultation with the Minister of Agriculture and Fisheries and is answered for in Parliament by Treasury Ministers. The expenditure of the Commission is borne on ordinary Votes of Parliament. Though the body has many characteristics in common with Government Departments, it enjoys a semi-independent status and requires little or no direction on political lines.

A similar body set up in 1941 is the War Damage Commission. It has greater independence than the Tithe Redemption Commission, though it is subjected by statute to Treasury "directions" on a number of general matters. It exercises considerable discretion, for example in deciding whether it is in the national interest when a building has been totally destroyed that a similar building should be erected on the same site. The activities of the Commission affect an enormous number of citizens, and where so much discretion enters into the settlement of so many claims it may help to gain public confidence if the work is entrusted to an independent body not directly geared to the Government machine. Obviously, no hard and fast rules can be drawn. It has been found in many similar fields that the work can be handled perfectly well by an ordinary Government Department; the Royal Warrants, for instance, leave a considerable amount of discretion to the Minister of Pensions in several types of exceptional case.

A more recent example of the same species of quasi-Government body is the Central Land Board set up under the Town and Country Planning Act of 1947. The Act extinguished all "development values" of land in private hands and created a fund of £300 million to compensate owners for their lost rights. Owners who wish to develop land or change its use may have to pay a "development charge" equal to the expected increase in the value of the land. The Board's primary function is to settle claims for payment out of the compensation fund and to levy the development charges. The Board, the membership of which is identical with that of the War Damage Commission, is subject to the general directions of the Minister of Town and Country Planning in the performance of its functions. The remuneration of the Board and its officers and all administrative expenses are defrayed out of monies provided by Parliament.

An earlier and more ambitious administrative experiment was the creation of the Unemployment Assistance Board under the Unemployment Act of 1934. The Board was appointed by the Crown and had a considerable degree of independence, though it operated with a Civil Service staff and all its expenses were borne on ordinary Parliamentary Votes except the salaries of the Board which, to stress its independence, were borne on the Consolidated Fund. Its duties were to draft Regulations for Ministers to submit to Parliament prescribing broad general scales of relief and then to apply the scales, exercising discretion in individual cases. The experiment was probably designed to achieve two objects, first, to ensure that scales of relief were framed by an authority which would not be subject to constant political pressure or to gusts of generous but thoughtless sentiment; secondly, to protect the Minister from responsibility for decision on the needs of every individual case and thus from an unmanageable spate of Parliamentary Questions.

163

In the early days the operations of the Board provoked a public controversy reminiscent of the ill-fated Poor Law Commissioners of 1834. There was in reality no sound analogy between the two bodies. The old Poor Law Commissioners had no responsibility to Parliament either direct or indirect. Their regulations were subject neither to approval nor to annulment by Parliament; the organisation they controlled consisted of a multitude of authorities with no corporate allegiance to any central authority, whereas the Assistance Board works through a Civil Service staff whose loyalty is to the Board and whose training imparts a proper respect for Parliament and an instinct for avoiding the embroilment of higher authority in political or other troubles. The initial controversy died down; time did its healing work and the Assistance Board continues as a feature of the Government's social administration. With the new title of National Assistance Board, it was given a fresh lease of life by the National Assistance Act of 1948. The Act extends the scope of national assistance to include financial assistance to all on proof of need, subject as was the case formerly to appeal to tribunals.

Another constitutional innovation, the Unemployment Insurance Statutory Committee, was also created by the Unemployment Act of 1934. The Committee's main function was to report annually on the financial position of the Unemployment Fund. If the Fund showed a surplus or a deficit, the Committee was bound to propose adjustments in contributions or benefits or both. The Minister was then bound to lay their proposals before Parliament and follow this up with a draft Order, to be approved by both Houses, proposing the adjustments recommended or other adjustments having the same financial effect. Thus the usual relationship between a Minister and a subordinate body was reversed. So far from the Minister controlling the body, it controlled him. What the Committee said about the Fund was binding on the Minister in default of fresh legislation.

The Committee was relieved of its statutory responsibility for the solvency of the Fund by Defence Regulations made in 1943 and the National Insurance Act of 1946 now vests control and management of the National Insurance Funds in the Minister; yet another function of Government pioneered by an extra-Governmental body has returned to the Governmental fold.

Entirely different in conception from these and other bodies of the financial type are the New Town Development Corporations established or to be established by the Minister of Town and Country Planning under the New Towns Act of 1946. The mere mention of them in the same context illustrates the baffling diversity of uses to which quasi-public bodies have been put in the last two decades. Like other quasi-public bodies, the New Town Corporations enjoy a semi-independent status, are subject to a measure of Ministerial control and have discretion in the handling of financial matters on behalf of the public. They have to plan the development of the new towns and communities and supervise the execution of their plans. They will exercise some of the functions of local government and will thus have similarities with Local Authorities. The members of the Corporations are appointed by the Minister, not elected—they could scarcely be elected by the citizens of towns yet unborn; but some are drawn from Local Authorities. Many of the functions of the Corporations are destined to pass one day to Local Authorities of one kind or another. The New Town Development Corporations, though temporary bodies, will also have affinities to the Public Corporations set up to manage industries and services described in Part 4 below. They can carry out services such as building houses, but they are more likely to arrange for services to be provided by private concerns or Local Authorities. Their function will be regulatory rather than managerial; and though they cannot ignore economic considerations, their main purpose is social rather than economic.

3. REGULATORY BODIES (INDUSTRIAL)

In the industrial field, many regulatory, as distinct from managerial, functions are being performed by quasi-Government bodies concerned with the administration of control or

165

assistance. In the years between the two World Wars, Government action often took the form of encouraging an industry to put its own house in order by means of a body of the guild type, representative directly or indirectly of different interests in the industry and equipped with statutory powers. In some cases, the administration of a levy on the industry or of a Government grant was included among the body's functions. In others, its powers were confined to securing compulsory amalgamations or to the administration of licensing systems and grading schemes.

The most important examples of the guild type were the Marketing Boards, like the Milk Marketing Board, set up under the Agricultural Marketing Acts of 1931 and 1933. The majority of each Board consists of representatives elected by the producers, but there are additional members appointed by the Minister from outside the industry. The purpose of the Boards was to protect home producers from disastrous falls in prices in an era of temporary glut and to help producers to help themselves by encouraging more efficient methods of marketing and production.

The Boards were set up under schemes which had to be approved by a majority of producers before the Minister presented them to Parliament for approval. The Boards have statutory powers of discipline over the producers covered by a scheme and there is provision for appeal to arbitration.

There are two features of the Agricultural Marketing Acts which are worth a passing mention, if only because they were the shadows of coming events. The first is the provision for the appointment by the Minister of Consumers Committees representing the various classes of consumer affected by the operations of a Marketing Board. A similar provision appeared in the Coal Mines Act 1930, of which more later. These Committees had no executive functions but they could refer complaints to the Minister who, in turn, could refer them to an impartial Committee of Investigation. The recent nationalisation measures for coal, transport, electricity and gas incorporate provisions for Consumers Committees of one kind or another. From time to time, Consumers Committees have been criticised

166

on two grounds. The first is that they are superfluous, since consumers are already represented in Parliament and can bring pressure to bear on the Minister through Parliamentary channels. The second is that Consumers Committees would not be likely effectively to safeguard the interests of consumers in their dealings with a powerful State monopoly. The first of these criticisms is theoretical and there is something to be said for taking the producer-consumer relation out of politics. The second criticism is a matter of speculation. Experience alone will show how effective the device of Consumers Committees will be. In the years immediately preceding the second World War, experience with the Agricultural Marketing Boards and similar organisations is not conclusive, because that was an era in which the supply of commodities in the markets of the world outran demand and producers even when armed with monopolistic powers were seldom in a position to exploit consumers. Since the War, experience of the newly nationalised industries has been too limited to enable firm conclusions to be drawn. The coal industry was the first large industry to be nationalised, but it has only been in public ownership for three years. It can be said, however, that the two Consumers Councils established under the Coal Industry Nationalisation Act to represent industrial and domestic consumers are performing a useful function. They can at any time bring grievances before the Minister for action, but their main purpose is to keep the Board fully attuned to the needs and wishes of the consumers of coal and to keep the consumers' representatives in touch with the Board's policies and difficulties.

Another interesting feature of the Agricultural Marketing Acts was the provision for Development Boards to operate joint schemes of development covering the producers of primary products and the processors of products manufactured from them. The scope of the Development Boards was thus wider than marketing alone and indeed embraced secondary production. The numerous functions of the Bacon Development Board, set up in 1935, with powers extended by the Bacon Industry Act 1938, included the licensing of bacon factories, the making and operation of factory rationalisation schemes, as

167

well as the administration of what was known as the "long contract system" for supplies of bacon pigs. This notion of Development Boards to some extent anticipated the idea of Development Councils for Industry which are being set up or are to be set up under the Industrial Organisation and Development Act of 1947.

The working of the Agricultural Marketing Acts and of the Boards set up under them has recently been reviewed by a Committee under Lord Lucas and their Report has been published by the Stationery Office; it is No. 48 of the Ministry of Agriculture and Fisheries Economic Series. The Government have since introduced a Bill[1] which seeks to amend the Agricultural Marketing Acts in several particulars.

The Wheat Commission (established under the Wheat Act of 1932) departed in many respects from the guild conception, but retained some features of it. The members were appointed by Ministers, but they were drawn largely from trade interests who were consulted about the appointments. Its task was to administer a scheme combining a levy on home-produced and imported flour with a subsidy on home-grown wheat designed to achieve stable returns to the growers. Intimate knowledge of the flour and corn trades was essential to the successful carrying out of this task and this was one reason for using a quasi-Government body of this kind. There were other reasons. The Commission was able to provide continuous expert and impartial supervision of the administration of the levy-subsidy scheme and could continue on a straight course unswayed by political breezes blowing from this quarter or that. Its constitution was such that it could command the confidence alike of the contributors and of the beneficiaries. The Minister of Agriculture, for his part, was freed from the burden of defending inside and outside Parliament decisions on scores of individual cases which otherwise might have congested the working of his Department. There was no Exchequer grant. An autonomous Wheat Fund was set up to be administered by the Wheat Commission. The Fund could not pay in subsidies more than it received in levies.

[1] Now the Agricultural Marketing Act, 1949.

Administration by a body not directly controlled by the Government in a case of this kind helps to bring home the fact that the purse, if there is one, is not bottomless. If there is extravagance in administration, there is so much less money available for distribution and the losers would be quick to see, through their representatives on the Commission, that energetic action was taken to check it.

Other commodity commissions for agriculture were set up in the years before the last war, but though their constitution was similar to that of the Wheat Commission, they did not have autonomous funds. On the contrary, their task was to administer Exchequer grants. Examples are the Land Fertility Committee set up under the Agriculture Act of 1937, and the Livestock Commission created by the Livestock Industry Act of 1937. Generally, the intention was that the Government should grant a subsidy but that the industry should adopt measures to make itself more efficient in the national, as well as in its own, interest. Where possible, commodity commissions were thus designed, like the Marketing Boards, to help the industries to help themselves.

Coal provides another example of how Government, at a time of dwindling markets and falling prices, made the grant of assistance, which took the form of quota regulation, the occasion for attempting to secure the reorganisation of an industry. Once Parliament said to Government "No tax without redress of grievances." Now Government said to industry "No assistance without improved efficiency." While, under the Coal Act of 1930, the coal industry organised its own bodies (central and local) for regulating quotas and for co-operative selling, a separate and independent body was set up, the Coal Mines Reorganisation Commission (which later became the Coal Commission), with the duty of encouraging amalgamations in the coal industry. Little progress was made in this field and the experience illustrates the difficulty of introducing, largely by consent, necessary but drastic reforms in an industry consisting of units independently owned and financed.

Cotton was another industry hit by the depression of the '30s and in need of reorganisation. The Cotton Spindles Board was set up under the Cotton Spinning Industry Act 1936, to enforce a policy of scrapping redundant spindles; it financed compensation to the owners by a levy on the spindles remaining in operation. In view of the need for a central body to co-ordinate sectional policies, a Cotton Industry Board was later created, on the initiative of the industry, by the Cotton Industry (Re-organisation) Act 1939. It has since been superseded by a post-war Cotton Board, the first of the Development Councils under the Industrial Organisation and Development Act 1947.[1] This Act is now one of the main instruments by which the Government seeks to regulate its relations with the private sector of industry. The new Cotton Board is, therefore, a landmark in a new field of constitutional development. The Chairman and two independent members of the Board are appointed by the President of the Board of Trade. In addition there are four members representing the employers and four representing the employees. The Board's compulsory powers are confined to the registration of all firms in the industry, the collection of levies (yielding not more than £250,000 a year) and the collection of information. For the rest, its functions are purely advisory. It cannot compel firms to carry out those things which it might wish to do. It is obliged to work in consultation with trade organisations and its success will therefore depend on the extent to which it gains and retains the industry's confidence.

The electricity industry provided yet another example of a quasi-Government body of the regulatory type. From 1919 onwards, it was evolving towards its present status of a national service, publicly-owned and operated. The Electricity Commission set up in 1919 was perhaps the first example of a statutory body nominated by the Government to supervise the operations of an industry. With the formation of the Central Electricity Board in 1926 to operate the grid system (see 4 below), the Electricity Commission had the task of supervising another quasi-Government body, namely the Board. Its super-

[1] Other Development Councils since set up are those for the furniture industry the jewellery and silverware industries, and the clothing industry.

vision extended to a large number of other electricity undertakings both private and municipal and the Commission was in turn subject to general directions by the Minister. A similar example is the Sugar Commission which controls certain activities of the British Sugar Corporation (see 4 below). The Bacon Development Board already referred to had power of direction over two Agricultural Marketing Boards, the Bacon Marketing Board and the Pigs Marketing Board. There are disadvantages in the use of tiers of quasi-Government bodies superimposed one upon the other; they tend unduly to complicate the administrative pattern and may be said to make control by Parliament and the people too remote. On the other hand, this kind of structure may be dictated by circumstances; it is a feature of the recent legislation for the nationalisation of transport.

This part of the story would not be complete without mention of financial corporations set up, not to provide outright grants as in the case of the Livestock Commission and some other of the commodity commissions already described, but to provide loan finance. When an industry or enterprise which is important to the national wellbeing has fallen on hard times or is for other reasons unable to secure from normal financial institutions the credit necessary for medium or long term development, the Government may find it convenient to set up a financial corporation to provide the credit facilities required. The first example again comes from agriculture. The Agricultural Mortgage Corporation (and a corresponding body in Scotland) were set up by Acts of 1928 and 1929 with Exchequer assistance to provide medium and long-term credits to farmers. This legislation superseded the Act of 1923 which authorised the Minister of Agriculture to encourage the creation of agricultural credit societies to whose finances the Exchequer made a 50 per cent. contribution. Another example was the Special Areas Reconstruction Association formed to give loans to industrialists, owning or intending to set up undertakings in the Special Areas, who could show that they had fair prospects of economic success but could not otherwise get credit on reasonable terms.

Then there are two institutions which might be described as quasi non-Government bodies, the Finance Corporation for Industry and the Industrial and Commercial Finance Corporation. These are privately-owned limited companies brought into being to serve the national interest; they maintain close relations with Government Departments and are virtually instruments of Government economic policy. The Finance Corporation for Industry was formed in 1945 by a group of insurance companies, trust companies and the Bank of England. Its function is the provision of short or medium-term finance for the rehabilitation and development of large industrial businesses which, for various reasons, are temporarily unable to obtain finance from normal sources. It has already operated in a wide field including iron and steel, oil, shipping, housing, hosiery and engineering. The Board of Directors consists of nine members chosen from persons "having experience in finance, commerce, industry, public administration and labour relations," a formula reminiscent of statutes establishing quasi-Government bodies. It is interesting to note how a body of this kind serving a public purpose, even when privately-owned and controlled, is similar in constitution and practice to a quasi-Government body set up by Act of Parliament. Although no Minister has formal powers of direction, in an indirect way Ministers can be made answerable to Parliament for the policy followed; if the Corporation were to get out of hand, Parliament could demand legislation enabling the Corporation to be controlled and Ministers would have to show cause why it should not be.

The Industrial and Finance Corporation was also set up in 1945, but in this case by the Joint Stock Banks and the Bank of England. It is similar to the Finance Corporation for Industry, but its function is to provide medium and long-term capital for small and middle-sized firms rather than large undertakings. Occasionally the Corporation provides "risk" capital by taking up preference or ordinary shares.

One general measure by which Government now seeks to regulate its relations with private industry has already been mentioned, i.e. the Industrial Organisation and Development

Act 1947 providing for the establishment of Development Councils. Of equal importance is the Restrictive Practices (Inquiry and Control) Act 1948 under which the Monopolies and Restrictive Practices Commission has been set up. Following the precedent of the Federal Trade Commission in the U.S.A. and the Combines Investigation Commission for Canada, labour practices are excluded from the scope of the Commission. The Monopolies Commission is primarily a fact-finding body, and it must report to the President of the Board of Trade on whom lies the responsibility for taking whatever action may be required in the first instance. The Commission does not initiate enquiries; it must be given a mandate from the Government, who thus retain in their hands the reins of a highly-strung animal set to run over a difficult course. The reasons for setting up the Commission are in part international, enabling the Government to fulfil an obligation under Chapter V of the International Trade Organisation Charter to suppress restrictive business practices. In part they are social: the national cake is not to be unfairly divided between monopolistic industries and those which consume their products; and in part they are economic, for if the Commission by eliminating restrictive practices secured an expansion of output in monopolistic industries, there would be a bigger national cake to divide. This would be in accordance with the tenet of orthodox economics that *perfect* competition in an *ideal* world creates the maximum of wealth for the community as a whole.

At first glance, the action of Government in curbing monopoly and encouraging free competition is inconsistent with the trend of Government intervention in the field of industry and commerce designed, in the case of many of the quasi-Government bodies so far described, to mitigate the effects of unbridled competition, and in the case of the quasi-Government bodies to be described in Part 4, to remove it altogether. The contradiction is more apparent than real. The world is far from being ideal and in the '30s when economic nationalism was rampant, it was necessary to cushion home industries from the full impact of the resulting economic crisis that beset the world. Moreover, competition is never "perfect" in the sense

173

required by orthodox economics; for some industries like railways there has for many years not even been an approximation to those conditions. Again, that it is uneconomic to leave industries like agriculture subject to uncontrolled seasonal variations has long been recognised and is in part the justification of policies pursued by successive Governments towards that industry. The final paradox is that for the nationalised industries which completely eliminate competition, the economic justification, apart from social and political considerations, of public ownership is that it may enable those industries to be shaped more nearly to the pattern dictated by free competition in a perfect world than would otherwise be possible. For example, the nationalised coal industry should be able to eliminate inefficient units of production and substitute for them modern and efficient units more rapidly than if the effects of competition, necessarily imperfect, were allowed to work themselves out, and more effectively than if a purely regulatory body (cf. experience of Coal Mines Reorganisation Commission) had the task of reorganising and reshaping the industry in private ownership in the face of opposition from financial interests. The Monopolies and Restrictive Practices Commission is thus seen to fit the general design of economic policy in the twentieth century.

4. MANAGERIAL BODIES

Before discussing the large trading and industrial corporations, a word should be said about quasi-Government bodies which, though managerial, are more concerned with things social than economic.

The National Assistance Board has been described earlier as a non-industrial regulatory body and its function is to exercise discretion in handling individual cases of hardship, but, as it has a nation-wide staff constituting what is virtually a national service, it almost qualifies for inclusion here. (This again illustrates the difficulty of achieving any classification of quasi-Government bodies in water-tight compartments.) National Insurance, on the other hand, at present lies wholly within the portfolio of a Government Department.

The new National Health Service is something of a hybrid. The Minister assumes full responsibility for supervising the Service and providing the hospital part of it. It is financed mainly out of monies voted by Parliament, and to a lesser extent from insurance contributions and local rates. Nevertheless, quasi-Government bodies of many kinds whose membership includes University teachers, hospital governors, representatives of the medical and other professions, and members of local health authorities, play an important part in the administration. In addition the Central Health Services Council with its associated Standing Advisory Committees composed of eminent members of the medical, dental, nursing, etc., professions, provide the Minister with expert and impartial advice on all the multifarious activities of the Service. Annual Reports by the Council on its own doings and those of the Advisory Committees must be submitted to the Minister and laid by him before Parliament.

The hospital services are run by Regional Hospital Boards working through Hospital Management Committees and by Boards of Governors of teaching hospitals. These bodies are subject to the directions of the Minister and draw their finance from him but they exercise considerable autonomy in planning, organising and supervising the services and in matters of day-to-day management.

The services rendered to the public by doctors and dentists in general practice and by pharmacists and opticians are "regulated" rather than "managed" by Executive Councils operating locally in areas which generally coincide with those of local health authorities. Each Executive Council appoints an Ophthalmic Services Committee which regulates on its behalf "supplementary ophthalmic services" rendered by doctors and opticians. The local health authorities themselves are woven closely into the administrative fabric of the National Health Service.

Applications to the Executive Councils from doctors who wish to join the Service are referred to another quasi-Government body, the Medical Practices Committee, which has the duty over the country as a whole of adjusting the distribution of doctors. The functions of this Committee are partly administrative and partly judicial, and an appeal lies to the Minister by any doctor who is refused admission to the Service. There is also the Dental Estimates Board for the whole country. Finally there is a quasi-judicial Tribunal which can remove inefficient doctors, dentists, pharmacists or opticians from the Health Service and from whose decisions an appeal lies to the Minister.

The Health organisation as a whole, for all its complexity, has evidently been constructed with a number of simple objectives in view: Ministerial responsibility at the centre; the need to harness professional skills and experience both to the higher direction of the Service and its local administration; the delegation of responsibility to local bodies; the fullest association of Local Authorities and other local interests and of professional bodies; and the greatest possible degree of independence for the practitioners of hitherto highly individualistic professions. Although the Minister is more intimately concerned with the working of the organisation than are Ministers in the case of other nationalised services, e.g. transport, it is noteworthy that over so large a field, quasi-Government bodies of one kind or another should be responsible for the day-to-day management and administration of the Health Service. Most of them appoint and employ their own staffs who do not belong to the Civil Service. Moreover, the doctors and dentists in general practice are neither employees of the Crown, nor of any authority set up under the Act. The arrangements indeed call to mind the guild-type of organisation exemplified by the Government's relationship with agriculture in the '30s. In some respects, the Agricultural Marketing Boards stand in the same relation to the producers as the Executive Councils to the doctors and dentists.

Between the social services and the nationalised industries, in a sort of no-man's land, is broadcasting. The British Broadcasting Corporation, set up in 1927 by Royal Charter, is in many ways the older brother of the big corporations later appointed under Act of Parliament to be in charge of national industries. Its origins, like theirs, were commercial. It purveys a marketable commodity—entertainment, though

176

as a side-line it conducts overseas services as the agent and at the expense of the Government. It is subject to Government direction, but enjoys a large measure of managerial freedom. It is expected to keep its expenditure on home broadcasting within the proceeds of the licence revenue raised on its behalf by the Government; and the entertainment value of its programmes must be such as to maintain this revenue. But although the Corporation must cut its coat according to its cloth and although it must pay some regard to the demands for its wares, its primary purpose is social and cultural. To some extent, the listeners and viewers get not what they are prepared to pay for but what the Corporation thinks it is good for them to hear and see. The consumers cannot in the nature of things freely choose, on the basis of a price schedule, between the various products offered by the Corporation nor, without paying the British licence fee, are they free to choose the products of other broadcasting systems in substitution.

With the B.B.C., as with the postal services, there is thus no question of using the price mechanism as a means of registering consumers' preferences or of obtaining the best distribution of productive resources. Does this mean that the B.B.C. as an institution is inherently undemocratic? An affirmative answer, if it were given, must be qualified in several ways. It has long been recognised that it is a function of Government to provide education. A child is compelled to go to school. He is not, in general, taught the subjects which his parents are willing to pay for, as the curriculum is determined by the school authorities; and adult education, if it is not compulsory, and if it affords a choice of subject to the student of continuation classes, is made available in forms determined not by the mechanism of price but by the dictates of authority. By the same token, should not the B.B.C. be free, as they are, to frame their programmes with one eye fully open to the desires of their fee-paying clients and the other half open to the possibilities of raising the level of taste? Moreover, with broadcasting, what is provided to-day has some bearing on what is demanded to-morrow. That appetite grows on what it feeds is shown by the striking growth in popularity in this country over the last 20 years of good music

M   177

and it is at any rate a possibility that the B.B.C. has played its part in creating this demand. A policy of preparing to meet the freely-expressed wishes of consumers in a few years time is not wholly undemocratic. Finally, there is no direct way of selling broadcasting to individual consumers so that each is free to buy or not to buy a particular item at a quoted price. The system adopted in some countries of selling space on the air to commercial advertisers is at best an indirect way of giving the consumers of broadcasting what they want.

For these reasons partly and because of a high level of efficiency and service, the B.B.C. has now become a British institution in fact as well as in name. The British public reserves the right to criticise as well as cherish the institutions which it takes to its heart. If the B.B.C. is not without its critics, it is nearly as well-established and as beyond serious controversy as earlier nationalised institutions like the Royal Navy.

The B.B.C. has arrived, and in getting there it has perhaps not had to trouble over-much about a problem which may be facing the new Corporations who are its younger brothers, i.e. public relations. A commercial concern advertises its wares for the best of business reasons and by this means can build up a measure of public goodwill. When, however, an industry is nationalised, there is in general no case for spending the public's money in persuading the public to buy goods from itself. Nor can a public corporation decently spend money on publicity designed to make itself popular with the public, though it has the duty of informing the public about its activities. The public can judge the corporations by their results, but their achievements and failures as an economic instrument of Government may be beyond the understanding of the many. And as people are apt to dislike what they do not understand and criticise what they dislike, the result may be to upset the morale of the nationalised industries just as the morale of an Army would be upset if the Generals were under a constant fire of uninformed criticism. For the B.B.C., the problem solves itself to the extent that broadcasting *is* public relations and for many the B.B.C. is identified with the friendly voice of an announcer or the microphone personality of a popular comedian.

Although the Central Electricity Board, established in 1926 to promote and control the bulk generation of electricity and develop bulk transmission lines, was closer than the B.B.C. in constitution and function to the large industrial corporations which were to come later, and although bodies like the Mersey Docks and Harbour Board, the Metropolitan Water Board and the Port of London Authority which evolved out of municipal rather than national enterprise were the true ancestors both of the B.B.C. and of the others, it was not until the advent of the B.B.C. that constitutional practice hardened into its present form. Successive Governments affirmed, confirmed and elaborated the doctrine that, whereas Ministers were responsible for the appointment of members of the Corporation and for changing the appointments if the Corporation were to become inefficient, the Corporation, and not they, were responsible for the day-to-day management of the Corporation's affairs, and Ministers accordingly were not answerable to Parliament for such details. This doctrine not only enables the Government effectively to delegate responsibility to the Corporations, but enables the latter in turn to delegate to subordinate formations. If the Corporations had to be in a position at short notice to provide the Minister with answers to give to Parliament on day-to-day questions of management arising throughout the country, the Headquarters of the nationalised industries would have to be expanded and the nightmare fantasy of "swollen staffs" (now easily dispelled by comparing published figures with those of other organisations) might become a reality. But what is organisationally desirable is not always constitutionally best. The autonomy of Public Corporations may mean better and more efficient management, but it also means less stringent Parliamentary control. If the doctrine is to stand the test of time, the Corporations must play their part, for example by furnishing the fullest information to the public through the medium of their Annual Reports which should disclose facts, whether favourable or unfavourable, as though their activities during the year had been continuously subject to Parliamentary question and answer.

After the Central Electricity Board and the British Broadcasting Corporation, came the London Passenger Transport Board, created in 1933. The constitution of that Board included a feature not repeated in later nationalisation measures. Appointments to the Board were made, not by the Minister, but by "Appointing Trustees" who included the Chairman of the L.C.C., the Chairman of the Committee of London Clearing Bankers and the Presidents of the Law Society and of the Institute of Chartered Accountants. The object of this method of appointing a Board was to eliminate risk of political bias. It is now, however, accepted doctrine that a Public Corporation set up to manage a business on behalf of the public should be responsible in the last resort through a Minister to Parliament, and Ministerial responsibility cannot be fully effective unless the Minister has the power to appoint the Board and, if he thinks them inefficient, to replace them.

In 1936 the British Sugar Corporation was formed. It, too, was *sui generis*, in that, although the Corporation was, to an extent, under public control, the equity remained in private hands.

In 1940, under an Act of Parliament passed the previous year, the British Overseas Airways Corporation was brought into being on what now must be regarded as orthodox lines. The Board was appointed by the Minister and was subject to his overhead directions on matters of policy. The Corporation was intended to operate on a commercial basis and eventually to pay its way. After the war, two more civil air organisations were established under statute, the British European Airways Corporation and the British South American Airways Corporation.[1]

The nationalisation of the Bank of England in 1946 calls for no comment. It made the Bank a Government agency in name as well as in fact. The Court of the Bank of England, like the Board of Governors of the B.B.C., are appointed by the King.

Another nationalisation measure a little out of the main stream of development is the Cable and Wireless Act, 1946, which transferred all the shares in Cable and Wireless Ltd. to Treasury nominees and replaced the Directors by those nomi-

[1] B.S.A.A.C. has now been absorbed in B.O.A.C.

nated by the Treasury. The organisation, however, remains in existence as a public company under the Companies Act and the intention is eventually to transfer the assets to the G.P.O.—another example of a quasi-Government body preparing the way for operation by a Government Department. The Act of Parliament setting up the Raw Cotton Commission for the purchase, importation and distribution of raw cotton is a reversion to the standard type. Members of the Commission are appointed by the President of the Board of Trade who may issue directions to them on matters affecting the national interest. The Commission are expected to pay their way.

There remain Coal, Electricity, Gas, Transport, Colonial Development and Overseas Food.

The first four are all basic industries under public ownership and as such have many problems in common—problems of organisation, of labour relations and of economics.

To some extent, the pattern of organisation of these industries has been pre-determined by the Acts of Parliament which created them. At the one extreme, the National Coal Board was given undivided responsibility for the organisation and conduct of the business of the nationalised coal mines, and it was left entirely free to set up its own subordinate organisation in the field: it delegates responsibility to Divisional Boards in charge of coalfields, appointed by the National Board and responsible to it, who, in turn, delegate to Area General Managers in charge of the basic units of management. At the other extreme, the Gas Act created 14 Area Gas Boards, each a Public Corporation in its own right, responsible for producing and distributing its products subject to co-ordination by the Gas Council, a federal body for the industry as a whole, having, in many fields, only limited power to act without the consent of the Area Boards. Electricity and transport are betwixt and between. The British Electricity Authority, like the National Coal Board, has undivided responsibility for the generation of electricity everywhere in the country (except in the area of the North of Scotland Hydro-Electric Board, created during the war and continued with little modification by the Electricity Act 1947). Distribution of electricity is in the hands of quasi-autonomous

Area Boards, appointed by the Minister, over which, however, the British Electricity Authority exercises a large degree of supervision.

For transport, there is the British Transport Commission, owning all the assets of the nationalised undertakings, superimposed on a number of executive agencies—the Railway Executive and the London Transport Executive, the Docks and Inland Waterways Executive, the Hotels Executive and the Road Transport Executive, appointed by the Minister.

If different principles of organisation have been adopted in the various nationalised industries, it is because, as the Lord President of the Council indicated during the Second Reading Debate on the Gas Bill,[1] the variations are preferable to a sealed pattern which would make it impossible to take into account the peculiar circumstances of the different industries or to establish in the light of experience which system of organisation was best.

The circumstances of these industries do, indeed, differ. In the case of coal, unlike gas, the marketing function knows no boundaries. The coal produced in one district can be sold in any other and, unlike both gas and electricity, can be exported overseas. In the marketing of coal, as in the operation of the centrally-controlled electricity grid, the greatest flexibility is required involving switches of supplies from one source of production to another. With costs varying from coalfield to coalfield, partly because of geological differences, capital development has to be planned to take place where costs of production and delivery to each market, at home and overseas, are least, and capital development must be centrally planned and co-ordinated more closely than in the case of gas. Moreover, in the present period of shortage and transition from wartime controls, it would not be possible suddenly to make each coalfield self-supporting without seriously upsetting other industries dependent on coal; and the National Coal Board, which has the duty of making the coal industry as a whole pay its way, must have direct responsibility for seeing that the constituent parts of the industry do everything possible to curb

[1] 11th February 1948. Hansard col. 480.

costs. It would be fallacious to assume that, because the Divisional Coal Boards have been set up by the National Coal Board and are not statutory corporations like the Area Gas Boards, there is greater centralisation in the coal industry than there would otherwise be. The central functions which fall to the National Coal Board would have to be performed whatever the statutory set-up, and if there were no National Coal Board to perform these functions for the industry as a whole, then the Minister would have to perform them. He would have to co-ordinate prices and selling, settle the apportionment of capital expenditure and hold each Divisional Board to account for the way in which they spent the coal consumers' money, contrasting and comparing the results achieved by the various Divisional Boards. This would, in fact, mean greater centralisation because the Minister, being answerable to Parliament in detail for any action taken in his name, would be unable to delegate as much managerial responsibility as the National Coal Board are able to do.

With electricity, too, because of the grid scheme, there must be central responsibility for the generation of electricity as there was in a large degree in the days of the Central Electricity Board. By contrast, the local distribution of electricity is largely a self-contained function and can thus be assigned to quasi-autonomous Area Boards. Local distribution of coal, so far from being undertaken by a central or regional authority, is not even nationalised.

Gas is different from both coal and electricity in that the Areas, whether considered as distributing or producing units, are largely self-contained.

The hierarchical organisation for transport reflects the special circumstances of the transport industries. The railways and road transport, for example, are in reality separate industries and would have independent corporations in charge of them were it not that the co-ordination of rail and road services is so much a matter of business management that it was necessary to superimpose the British Transport Commission to assume the higher management rôle. It is true that the duty of co-ordinating the fuel and power industries, i.e. coal, electricity and gas, is left in part to the Minister of Fuel and Power and in part to the industries themselves, but there is less need for close and continuous co-ordination than in the case of the transport services.

There has been some discussion of late about the organisation set up by the various Public Corporations within the statutory frame-work. Organisation is a means to an end and though it is important, its importance should not be exaggerated. The strength of a hand at bridge depends more on the cards which are held than on the way they are sorted into suits. No amount of shuffling of cards will turn a bad hand into a good. Similarly, no amount of coloured charts can do anything for an organisation if the men who fill the posts are lacking in capacity. The men in an organisation and what they do will always be more important than the precise form of the organisation. The Public Corporations have drawn, and are drawing constantly, on the experience of other large-scale business organisations, though it is only the experience of the very largest in this country and in the United States, and of Governmental organisations like the Service Departments and the General Post Office, which is truly relevant. They are also, day-by-day, learning much from their own unique experience of the problems of large-scale organisation in the new context of nationalisation. For reasons which will be discussed later, the ends of the nationalised industries in the fields of labour relations and economic policy are not precisely comparable with those of large business monopolies, nor, in general, of Government Departments responsible for the conduct of national services. Since organisation cannot usefully be considered apart from the ends which it is intended to serve, the Public Corporations, as time goes on, will look more and more to their own practical experience and that of other Public Corporations for enlightenment and guidance.

Meanwhile, much good can come from public discussion and exchange of views on the problems of large-scale organisation. Unfortunately, however, public controversy has concentrated on subjects which, though most debated, are least debatable. Is it contended that between a central authority and its operating units there should be no intermediate formations? A negative answer is at once suggested by the experience of large commercial organisations like I.C.I., Unilever and General Motors and of Governmental organisations like the General Post Office and the Armed Forces of the Crown. Is it contended that in a large business there should be no departments or that at National Headquarters there should be no central advisory and consultancy services, allowing an organisation, say, to employ one taxation expert at Headquarters of the highest calibre instead of 50 such experts dotted about the country? Is it contended that the heads of departments, even if they are dubbed "functional," should in no circumstances be appointed to the Board of Management? Experience of other organisations again suggests a negative answer. Most of the controversy can, in fact, be reduced to a single question based on an impossible premise—how can a big business be run so as to be entirely unlike any other big business, national or private? Then there is an assertion that it is important to devolve authority and responsibility so as to give the greatest encouragement to local initiative and to do this in such a way as to maintain a clear line of command. This is rather like asserting that the earth is not flat. There is no-one who could be found to deny it inside Public Corporations or outside. The real problem is to reconcile the conception of a clear line of command with the need for carrying out through specialist departments the work of large businesses. One solution of the problem, well-known and beyond the area of debate, lies in the system known as "line-and-staff," which is a feature of comparable Government and commercial organisations. It involves a clear line of command and responsibility, with specialist staff serving each body or person in the line of command. The system is not unknown to the National Coal Board, who adopted it in the early days of its existence long before someone invented a myth of functional tubes stretching from London to the pits down which passed an unending stream of conflicting instructions !

There is a temptation to dismiss the whole question of organisation as a great irrelevancy and to say with Pope:

"For forms of government let fools contest:
Whate'er is best administered is best."

But there are many organisational problems confronting Public Corporations which remain unanswered or have only been partially answered by the experience of the past. Here are some of them:—

    (i) *Not* whether all functional boards are good or all functional boards are bad, but *in what circumstances* is it desirable to have heads of departments on Boards of Management or to have a Board which blends functional and non-functional responsibilities? How far are these questions of organisation and how far are they questions of personalities?

    (ii) In what circumstances should there be a Board at all? All quasi-Government bodies have hitherto been composed of groups of people having collective responsibility. This may have been due to the need to harness diverse experience, to create the appearance as well as the fact of impartiality— there is safety in numbers—and to achieve greater independence of Government than might be possible if, instead of a collective body, a single individual were entrusted with the responsibility. It is not surprising that some of the creations of quasi-Government bodies should themselves be Boards of Management like the Divisional Boards set up by the National Coal Board. The commercial precedent of subsidiary companies is also relevant. In what circumstances is it best to have a subordinate Board of Management and in what circumstances is it best to have a single person in sole command of the organisation, like a commander-in-chief?

    (iii) What is the rôle in a nationalised industry of the non-specialist administrator accustomed to dealing with broad problems of national policy, to looking outwards as well as inwards and possessing a sense of the fitness of things social, economic and political? Should these be specially trained and recruited with a view to filling the most responsible posts in the organisation (*c.f.* the Administrative Cadet Scheme of the Railways)? Or should technicians, e.g. colliery managers, be put through a course at a staff college in order to make administrators of them (*c.f.* the practice of the Fighting Services)?

(iv) On what lines should relations *between* Public Corporations develop? If it is convenient and economical for them to do some things in common, e.g. co-ordination of recruitment or of purchasing procedure, how can this be brought about without subjecting them to over-rigid central controls? If there are disputes between Corporations, can they only be resolved by Ministers, who are the ultimate custodians of the national interest, or should there be tribunals to give impartial and non-political decisions?

(v) Similarly, how should relations between Corporations and Government Departments develop? Should Government Departments and Corporations undertake services in common for the sake of economy, or is it essential to prevent the clogging of the Government machine that the Corporations should operate with complete independence? Or, to take a small example, is it now anachronistic that a Public Corporation, say an Electricity Board, should be prosecuted by the Crown for breach of a safety regulation when the outcome is that the public impose a fine on themselves; or is this a useful procedure for bringing home to the Boards their special responsibilities and for marking irregularities with publicity?

(vi) In what ways is it possible to adapt the organisation of the nationalised industries so that they may be more truly an expression of the democratic spirit underlying so many of our institutions? If, as has been suggested, industries should be "localised" rather than nationalised, and made subject to local government authorities instead of the national Government, two other questions arise. How would it be possible to pursue a national policy for prices, investments and wages without involving a system of dual control? And how should Local Government itself be reshaped to assume these large and vital responsibilities? Alternatively, if the real "constituents" of the local producing units of the nationalised industries are the workers at those units and consumers everywhere, not only those in the locality, is there any virtue in making local boards of management of publicly-owned industries subject to the control of local government authorities, however reformed? Should not the democratising influence be looked for, not so much in a close link with local government, but in joint consultative committees between management and workers and in consumers' committees such as are provided for in the statutes setting up the Public Corporations?

The last question goes beyond the field of organisation into the field of labour relations. Are labour relations, like organisation, only a means to an end, the creation of the maximum of wealth for the community? They are certainly a means to that end, but when many millions of citizens spend their working lives in the employ of Public Corporations, their working conditions, and the satisfaction they are able to get as craftsmen or the sense of achievement in contributing to the good of the community, must be regarded as ends in themselves. In labour relations, nationalisation has brought new difficulties and new opportunities. In providing incentives for management, the prospect of a career of service and responsibility must take the place of the remoter, but to some more glittering, prospect of becoming a captain of industry and making a personal fortune. The relations between management and workpeople are all-important. Two assumptions are often lightly made. The first is that before nationalisation everyone worked enormously hard because of the profit motive. If "wage-earners" is substituted for "everyone," the proposition becomes patently absurd. The other assumption is that once the profit motive was removed and men felt that they were working not for the benefit of individual shareholders but for the community at large, they would at once put every ounce of effort into their work. Unfortunately, this has not, so far, been proved by experience. That is not to to say that many men serving the nationalised industries are not responding fully to the new stimuli of public service, but there is still a fund of latent energy and goodwill and the Public Corporations have the duty of finding means of releasing it for the benefit of the community. The institutional machinery is already there. Joint consultation between management and men in the workshops and in the pits has been created where it did not exist before nationalisation and the workpeople can feel that they are playing their part with management in ordering their own working lives. Meanwhile, everything is being done to develop in the managers initiative, responsibility and sense of leadership. It is less a matter of organisation than of human relations, of esprit de corps and of morale, a matter of attitudes of mind, of the growth of mutual confidence and responsibility between management and men and the laying aside of old prejudices and old inhibitions.

If the human problems facing the Public Corporations are more novel and complex than the problems of organisation, so also are their economic problems. Unlike the monopolistic organisations which preceded them it is not sufficient that they should price their products and services so as to yield a given return on their capital; they must have a structure of prices and rates based as far as possible on the costs, or marginal costs, of producing individual items and individual services, to encourage consumers to take more of what is cheaply produced and less of what is dearly produced and to encourage industrialists to site their works as near as possible to the sources of production. It is axiomatic that consumers should be free to choose between the various kinds of goods and services on offer, and the only way to prevent a waste of national resources on a large scale is to use the price mechanism in this way to guide their choice. Put in other words, not only should the nationalised industries as a whole pay their way without subsidy, as the statutes which created them provide, but each part—each activity in each area—should as far as possible pay its way. Thus, the principle adopted by Parliament for whole industries would be applied by the Corporations themselves, gradually it may be, to smaller and smaller sub-divisions of these industries.

In the field of capital development, too, new problems will have to be met and solved. The industries will have to be expanded well beyond the point at which expansion would cease if they were commercial monopolies bent only on making the maximum profit. Yet they must not expand so far that the additional goods and services are provided at a loss, even though the books of the industry as a whole can be made to balance, as this would denote mis-application of national resources. A new commercial technique, based possibly on a new technique of accountancy, is required.

Wages policy poses similar problems. Prices, investments and wages indeed form a trio of inter-dependent problems. Their solution may entail wages differences for men doing the same work in different places. This may be unavoidable if wages are to be an incentive for men to move from one employment to another where their labour is most fruitful in adding to the nation's wealth. For the Unions, this may mean a break with past tradition. The formulation of a new wages policy, possibly written into the terms of reference of Arbitration Tribunals, will make great demands on the foresight of the Corporations and on the powers of leadership and sense of responsibility of the Unions and will call for the highest statesmanship from both.

In all this economic management of the affairs of nationalised industries, new qualities and a new outlook are needed for the higher direction. With a private business, the operations of which are not large enough to influence the market price of its products, management can pursue a policy of seeking to maximise profits without seriously disturbing the distribution of the nation's current resources and without the capacity for incurring large-scale waste. With the nationalised industries, the opportunities are there not only for increasing the national wealth beyond what was possible under private ownership, but also, be it said, for running down the economic activity of the country below what was formerly possible. The principle of personal gain which actuates private industry must, therefore, give way to a philosophy of serving the public interest by a strict application of economic policies. These policies must be simplified and "vulgarised" until they are fully understood by all who have to apply them and conform to them, management and workpeople alike. The standard of living of *all* the people depends on the success with which this is done.

The full exploitation of home resources, in which the home Public Corporations have their part to play, is intended to go hand-in-hand with efforts to increase the productivity of un-developed or little-developed territories overseas in the interests of the people of those territories, of this country and indeed of the world. The two Public Corporations set up under the Over-seas Development Act, 1948, the Colonial Development

Corporation and the Overseas Food Corporation, are the instruments of this policy. The Colonial Development Corporation operates exclusively in British Colonies, but it is not concerned exclusively with food and agricultural production. The Overseas Food Corporation is not confined to the Colonies, but its activities are confined to food and agricultural production. There is an apparent over-lapping of functions in Colonial territories which in practice will be resolved as follows. The Overseas Food Corporation will be concerned mainly with large schemes beginning from virgin soil, while the main work of the Colonial Development Corporation will be to promote and develop forms and methods of production already well-established. These Corporations are similar in constitution, in scope and in structure to the home Public Corporations already described. They are, however, the instruments of colonial policy as well as of economic policy, and their establishment is a corollary to the Colonial Development and Welfare Acts of 1940 and 1945 which foreshadowed the development of public utilities in the Colonies and improved Government and social services. In part, too, these Corporations will act as finance houses, providing capital finance which would not otherwise be available, and in this respect are similar to the purely financial Corporations, like the Agricultural Mortgage Corporation and the Finance Corporation for Industry. Though they will conduct a number of activities themselves, either directly or through the medium of subsidiary companies, their function is to supplement rather than supplant private enterprise. Some operations of the Colonial Development Corporation have already been made public.[1] It has lent money to British Guiana Consolidated Gold Fields Co.; it plans also to participate in forestry development in British Guiana and in association with two privately-owned companies it has set up a body to prepare a plan of operations. It has already purchased a timber concession in the Colony. The Corporation is developing an egg and poultry farm in Gambia, from which

[1] Further information about the Colonial Development Corporation and the Overseas Food Corporation has since been made available in their Annual Reports and Accounts for 1948 and 1948-49 respectively.

in two or three years it is hoped to produce 20 million eggs annually and a million pounds of poultry for export. 10,000 acres of land there have been leased and scheduled for clearance. The Overseas Food Corporation has been engaged in the East Africa Groundnuts Scheme.

The possibilities before the Corporations are immense, though they have many difficulties to overcome, particularly in the early years of their existence. Schemes for growing tropical grain crops, citrus fruits, etc.; for rearing cattle, pigs and poultry; for timber production; for development of fisheries; for the mining of iron, copper, lead, bauxite, coal, gold, etc., are no doubt on the agenda for future developments. Manufacturing and processing undertakings to complement the production of primary materials would follow. Thus, whatever the present difficulties, these Overseas Corporations, which are perhaps linear descendants of the East India Company, are opening a new chapter of British enterprise and endeavour.

The parish of British quasi-Government bodies is now, indeed, as wide as the world and in this short sketch it has not been possible to do justice to a subject ranging from quasi-Government bodies used as extensions of the normal functions of Government to those shaping the destinies of industries and people at home and overseas. Many quasi-Government bodies have had to go without even a passing reference—the Race Course Betting Control Board, the Air Registration Board, the Herring Industry Board, the Miners' Welfare Commission, the Forestry Commission, the Agricultural Land Commission, the three Iron and Steel Corporations dealing with salvage, scrap and disposals, and many others too numerous, though not by any means too unimportant, to recount. At a time when quasi-Government bodies are daily being adapted to fresh uses, it would be premature and dangerous to draw final conclusions. One can only indicate a possible trend here and ask a question there. Later, many years later, history will pass judgment.

LOCAL GOVERNMENT

by J. H. WARREN, M.A., D.P.A.

I. INTRODUCTORY

THE general aim of this chapter may be stated quite shortly. It is to review the changes which have taken place in the scope and system of English Local Government over a period extending from the eve of the first world war until the morrow of the second. The field is vast, the changes many, and the standpoints for such a review widely different. At the outset of what can only be a selective study, and not a panoramic survey, we must therefore specify more closely the aspects of local government on which our interest is to fasten.

One standpoint from which we might consider its scope would be to mark out the contributions it has made to our civilisation in general, or to successive phases of national need, such as civil defence in war-time, or housing in the interludes of peace. We could recall the part it has played in pioneering or establishing new public services. We could illustrate its impacts on the life of the citizen, and the extent to which it has served his needs and well-being. Although a complete history of *modern* local government (since 1834) remains to be written, it is certain that all that it has accomplished in these ways, both before 1914 and since, would make an astonishing story. But a review from this standpoint is largely beside our purpose; and to attempt to take even snapshots from it would be futile, unless these were to penetrate, as they cannot, to the vast background before our chosen period of thirty odd years.

If we are concerned with the scope of local government, it is as a category, or perhaps several categories, of administrative function, falling to be discharged by the agencies of local government as distinct from other agencies of government or public service. In reciting the changes it has suffered, it is the changing balance between local government responsibility and the responsibility of these other agencies which is our main interest. As to the system in its other aspects, our concern is not with the constitution, or the administrative practice, of the individual organ of local government, but with the structure and layout of local government as a whole, and with its relationship, administrative and financial, to the central executive organs of the State.

An interest which fastens upon aspects such as these is, in essence, a political one, directed to the general "displacement" of local government in the national polity, and to the rôle it is playing, or should be made to play, in democratic government and public service. It has been our national belief that democracy should be local as well as central, and that what we call local government should always represent a substantial measure of local *self*-government and be something different from the decentralised activity of the State machine. All our political philosophers aver that democracy can only rest upon a firm foundation of local government in this sense of the term. As a consequence, it has been generally agreed that we should always keep on foot a suitable standing structure of local self-government to which appropriate functions can be assigned from time to time. Nineteenth-century experience taught us that such a standing structure was infinitely preferable, on grounds of economy and administrative efficiency, to a policy of creating ad hoc bodies for varying needs as they arose. But behind the legislation of 1888-94 which completed such a standing structure lay the broader political idea that it was a cardinal and salutary principle to maintain a permanent and commodious repository of local power—as an alternative to the undue extension of the bureaucratic arm of the state, and as a means of providing the widest opportunity for practical education in political responsibility.

The period under review—chosen to conform with the general design of this book—is one in which, after a long epoch of freedom and expansion, the situation of local government changes materially. New central agencies, notably of the kind we·call public corporations, are established, to undertake new services, or to replace the agencies of local government. Considerable transfers of function take place from smaller to larger geographical units in the existing local government structure, and even the word "local" thus takes on a new significance. Central control over local government expands and tightens, and is accompanied by immeasurably enlarged assistance from central funds. For these reasons, the political interest of local government during the period is considerable; the changes being of a kind which obviously invite us to review them in the light of the philosophy on which local government was built up.

Political principle, however, must always be conditioned by administrative considerations. This, in fact, is one of the truths which the events of the period re-inforce. The particular sphere to be assigned to local self-government is not a question which is, or wholly cán be, determined by considerations of democratic freedom and responsibility, viewed as capable of development by ties of neighbourhood and the activity of local communities; or even by the consideration that local self-government is an educative process and invaluable to democracy on that account alone. The assignment of local government functions must have some regard to administrative considerations. What lends to the period under review its special significance is the emergence of a situation in which the content of local government becomes more and more affected by administrative considerations, and in which these themselves no longer turn, as they largely did in the nineteenth century, upon the non-availability of other feasible agencies than "local authorities" for the conduct of public services, or upon a simple choice between the assignment of services to State departments on the one hand or the agencies of local self-government on the other. There is rich pasture therefore for our accompanying interest— the administrative one.

We cannot pretend to enumerate all the factors, or to strike the particular equations, which have determined this or that particular change. What we shall try to do is to show the main differences, in scope and shape, between local government in 1914 and local government in 1949, and to indicate the reasons, and the underlying social and economic pressures, which brought these changes about.

2. FUNCTIONS

The functions for which local authorities were responsible in 1914 could be divided, as they can still be divided to-day, despite growth here or shrinkage there, into four broad groups. The first group, of Police or Protective Services, as we may call them, has hardly altered in range; and comprises police, fire brigade, and ambulance services, and the administration of a mass of detailed regulations for the suppression of nuisances, the regulation of building, and the observance of weights and measures, and standards of purity in food and drugs. Broadly speaking, the same is true of the second group, which we may call the Communal Services, because they are used by all as needed, and paid for through local taxation, and which comprise a variety of environmental services characteristic of, and essential to, urban life: the maintenance of roads and streets, the provision of sewers and means of sewage disposal and treatment, the collection and disposal of household refuse, and the provision of public cleansing, public lighting, parks, open spaces, public baths, and burial grounds. We must, however, note important changes which occurred between the two wars in the control and provision of highways. The Local Government Act of 1929 effected a substantial re-shuffle of responsibilities outside the county boroughs by transferring the responsibility for control and finance from the borough and district councils to the county councils, with provision for the larger of the urban authorities of the county areas to exercise powers of delegation and agency. But these changes left highways still within the scope of local government. In 1936, however, was passed the Trunk Roads Act. This measure established a national network of trunk roads under the control of the Ministry of Transport, to be maintained at national expense. For all roads chosen as the initial net-work of trunk routes, and for any future improvements or new national routes, the local authorities thus ceased to be responsible, though the counties or larger town authorities are used by the Ministry as agents for maintenance and improvement in the sections passing through their areas. The sections of trunk road in the county boroughs, i.e. the larger towns, were excepted from the Act of 1936 but have since been brought in by the Trunk Roads Act 1946, making additions to the net-work.

Both the first and second groups of services being intimately connected with environmental layout and control, we may conveniently note here the greater powers given to the Local Authorities by a succession of Planning Acts in 1919, 1932, 1942, 1943, and 1947. The Act of 1932 provided for a widened concept of environmental planning from "Town" to "Town and Country"; and the Act of 1947 dealt with the problems of compensation and betterment which had rendered preceding legislation almost nugatory.

It is in the remaining two groups—the Social and Trading Services—that the greatest changes have taken place, though in contrasted ways. The history of the Social Services throughout the period is one of vast expansion, marked, however, in the years immediately following the close of the second war, by a heavy transfer of responsibilities from the local authorities to new agencies. We may count Education, Poor Law, and Housing as nuclear constituents of the group in 1914; but although the history of the education service is one of development rather than startling changes in scope, and of re-orientations of policy which still remain to be realised under the Education Act of 1944, the situation amounts to much more than this in Housing and Poor Law. In 1914 even the largest and most progressive authorities could point to only a few municipal houses, built, mostly, under the limited powers of the Housing of the Working Classes Act 1890. "The Housing Problem" arose in its acute form after the war of 1914-1918, partly through the suspension of building during the war but mainly through conditions accumulating over a long period. To meet it Parliament passed a succession of measures, most of them making subsidies available in one form or another. The Addison Act of 1919 made a start with building by local authorities on a substantial scale; the Chamberlain Act of 1923 assisted both local authorities and private enterprise; the Wheatley Act of 1924 continued subsidies on a new scale to local authorities alone; while the Greenwood

Act of 1930 concentrated on slum clearance and the Young Act
of 1935, on the relief of overcrowding. These, coupled with
measures to cope with a recrudescence of the problem after the
war of 1939-45, have made most local authorities owners of
large housing-estates, the rent-rolls of the cities often numbering
upwards of 50,000 houses, and places like Wythenshawe
(Manchester) being in effect municipally-built towns.

As to the Poor Law, the service had been locally administered
(with a strong infusion of central control) since 1834, though the
agents in 1914 were still the ad hoc Boards of Guardians. In
1929 their functions were transferred to the county and county
borough councils. Since it was necessary, in abolishing the ad
hoc poor law authorities, to make some provision for the work
of valuation for rating, which had been in their hands as raisers
of the first local rates, i.e. the Poor Rate, the Rating and
Valuation Act 1925 had, in anticipation, entrusted this work
to the borough and district councils, with provision for appeal
to local assessment committees, and established central and
county valuation committees with certain rights to intervene.
in pursuance of uniformity of valuation. The changes took
place when the policy advocated by the Webbs' Minority
Report of the Poor Law Commission of 1909 had gained much
ground. One aspect of this policy encouraged the local authorities to develop the Poor Law infirmaries as General Hospitals,
to be conducted like those which a few authorities had provided under an enabling provision in the Public Health Acts;
and the local authorities thus came to be hospital authorities
side by side with the voluntary bodies providing similar institutions. On the other hand the financial strain of providing
out-relief for the able bodied unemployed in the great economic
depression which arose between the two wars powerfully reinforced the philosophy of "break-up," and brought about
in 1934 the transfer of the local authorities' responsibility for
financial assistance to the unemployed to a newly created
Assistance Board.

Keeping for the moment to the expansive phase, a further
feature of the period after 1914 was the rise of a variety of
personal and clinical, as distinct from environmental, health

services. On very limited lines, a school meal service had been started in 1906, a school medical service in 1907, and arrangements for the detection and treatment of tuberculosis in 1912. In the years immediately after the first world war these grew immeasurably, both as regards the kind of provision made and the sections of the population catered for. Considerable development also took place in the care of mental defectives, a service inaugurated in 1913. In 1918, following upon an experimental start under the Notification of Births Act 1915, the Maternity and Child Welfare Service was established. And in 1920 the Blind Persons Act inaugurated a service for the care of the blind.

From even the thumb-nail sketch just given we can see well enough how matters stood in 1939. Apart from national health and unemployment insurance, panel doctoring, and the relief of the able-bodied unemployed, the social and health services, apart from voluntary provision, rested with the local authorities. The last two or three years since the conclusion of the second world war have brought drastic change. When public opinion accepted, during the second world war, the idea of a comprehensive National Health Service, there was a general expectation that the local authorities would be the main agencies to administer it; but the scheme eventually embodied in the National Health Service Act of 1946 was cast on vastly different lines. Not only was the responsibility for the supervision of the General Practitioner Service placed in the hands of special mixed bodies. What was more surprising was that the hospitals were placed in the hands of ad hoc Regional Boards. So far from taking over voluntary hospitals the local authorities lost their own: i.e. those "general" hospitals which some of them had established under the Public Health Act, the specialised hospitals which they had established for the treatment of infectious disease, the Poor Law infirmaries they had taken over in 1929 and developed as general hospitals "appropriated" to uses going beyond the ambit of the Poor Law, and even the maternity homes they had established under the Maternity and Child Welfare Act of 1918. Following upon the National Health Service Act 1946, came the National Assistance Act 1948, designed to achieve the final "break-up" of the Poor Law. This transferred remaining local authority responsibilities for out-door relief to the Assistance Board and placed under the control of the Board new forms of institutional care for classes previously dealt with under the Poor Law, the result being that little if anything remained to the local authorities of the functions they had inherited in 1929.

By way of set-off against the loss of functions we have described, both the Acts mentioned entrusted some new responsibilities to the local authorities, either to establish services of a new kind, or to expand and re-orientate existing ones. The National Health Service Act directed them to establish domici-liary nursing and welfare services, as ancillary services to those under the control of the new ad hoc central regional and local machinery for hospital and medical services. And the National Assistance Act directed them to inaugurate an improved service for providing accommodation, with accompanying care and welfare services, for the aged and infirm, and such special groups as the blind, deaf, and dumb. A new Children Act of 1948 also directed the local authorities to proceed with a rehabi-litation of existing arrangements for the care of children lacking parental care. Important as these new responsibilities are, they are not regarded by the local authorities as balancing the responsibilities they have lost; and indeed there can be no doubt that the loss of so many major institutions and the cutting out of the local authorities from so much institutional responsibility represents a very drastic reduction of their rôle in the conduct of Social Services.

It is in the fourth group of services, however—that of the Trading Services as they are called—that the local authorities have suffered the most drastic loss of functions; a loss they feel the more keenly because the services lost were ones which they took over from private enterprise, or themselves pioneered, upon their own, and not a central, initiative. The characteristic of these Trading Services is that they are run on a self-supporting basis, by charging the consumers a commercial price according to individual use or consumption; any net surplus being applied in reduction of price, or, in a limited measure, towards relief of rates or to a "common good" fund for general local amenities. Apart from some peculiar local enterprises such as the owner-ship and operation of docks, as at Bristol, telephones, as at Hull, or bridges, as at Runcorn, the services most commonly under-taken by municipalities on this footing were the provision of gas, water, electricity, and local street transport. The muni-cipalities had established themselves in these fields of economic enterprise well before 1914, not so much by general legislation as under local powers granted by Parliament on an extending scale throughout the nineteenth century. Gas and water supply they had for the most part (though not everywhere) taken over from the private companies which had originated the supplies; but electricity they had in many areas pioneered themselves, from the rise of the industry in the eighteen-eighties. The same was largely true of the electric street tramway systems to which the horse-drawn vehicles of the eighteen-seventies gave way.

It is important to note, however—for the fact goes far in itself to explain recent changes in these spheres—that neither in 1914 nor afterwards did the municipalities occupy the whole of any one of the four fields. They had got very close to this in water supply; and as matters stand to-day privately owned water undertakings are the exception rather than the rule and are mostly small units serving small communities. At the close of the second world war little more than a third of the gas industry, measured by output, was in municipal hands, the metropolis being supplied by three large companies, built up by successive amalgamations, whose size more than compensated for the preponderant position of the municipalities in the substantial towns of the provinces. In the field of electricity supply the municipalities predominated, and accounted for two-thirds of the output, notwithstanding that, in 1902, municipalisation had suffered the first check in its mounting career in these fields by the formation of a number of Power Companies, established to furnish bulk supplies over areas not then developed and of a size and configuration transcending the local limits charac-teristic of both municipal and ordinary company supply. As to the fourth field, local street transport, the local authorities were practically in exclusive occupation in 1914. But already in that year the impact of the new form of propulsion, the petrol engine, was being felt. One or two local authorities had already taken powers to supplement tramway services by omnibus services and were beginning indeed to substitute one for the other. Some of them obtained powers to run in peripheral territories, or to link town with town. But in the absence of any general legislation regulating the change-over to a form of propulsion which was no longer tied to strictly local limits of operation, the period from 1914 to 1930 was one of disorderly competition for inter-town and long-distance running rights, and, to some extent indeed, for running rights within existing tramway limits. It was a competition among companies, among municipalities, and as between the one kind of entrepreneur and the other. The Road Transport Act of 1930, passed to deal with this situation, established Traffic Commissioners with a duty to assign routes, eliminate wasteful competition, and regulate fares; and after some years their work secured a measure of order and co-ordination. But in the result the municipalities had seriously lost ground. Free of the boundary considerations that affected the municipalities, the companies were found to have entered the inter-town and long-distance branches of the new service in strength, and the effect of the Act of 1930, therefore, was inevitably (short of nationalisation or a re-assignment of local government responsibilities) to consolidate their position.

What has been said of transport is a pointer to a general characteristic of all four trading services as they had grown up in the nineteenth century and as they existed in 1914; a characteristic which, again, is directly relevant to recent changes. All four services existed in 1914 in the form in which they had grown up in the previous half-century or more: local monopolies, locally managed, with "markets" based, for the most part, on the town communities which the services had sprung up to supply. The rural communities (then rural in a sense no longer true of so many of them to-day) had not previously been catered for, though outlying services were being developed by the town-based undertakers. Developments in the field of electricity supply between the two wars illustrate in a more pronounced form a process which began to affect all these services in one way or another. Impelled by a changed conception of these services as no longer local amenities, but essential forms of national economic provision, a process sets in of fitting the local monopolies on which the services rested into some framework of national planning, supervision, or control, in order to realise the implications of the new conception. The Report of the Williamson Committee in 1919 drew attention to the fact that technical advance allowed of the generation of electricity upon a large scale and its transmission over wide areas, whereas the industry remained organised in the small units and areas with which it had begun, the result being uneconomic generation in small and inefficient stations, a higgledy-piggledy routing of transmission, and different systems of frequency and pressure in the distribution of supplies to the consumer. The measure introduced into Parliament was designed to effect a radical reorganisation of the industry by the establishment of Joint Electricity Authorities to generate and distribute over fairly wide areas; but the House of Lords struck out the provisions enabling the Joint Authorities to secure the transfer of the undertakings, company or municipal, which it was proposed to integrate in areas marked out by an Electricity Commission; and the resulting Electricity Act of 1919 remained a dead letter, except for the establishment of a highly competent technical body, the Electricity Commission. There was, as we have seen, a divided ownership of the industry. The prevailing political sentiment was not prepared on principle to countenance the expropriation of company undertakers. The municipalities themselves resisted absorption by new bodies, especially since these might be representatives of companies brought into the "mixed" Joint Authorities.

A new Electricity Act of 1929 made a new and ingenious approach to the problem. It side-stepped the issue of company-v-municipal ownership by imposing common limitations on both which would secure a better footing for generation and main transmission, judged to be the more important elements in the problem. Generation would be concentrated in large "selected stations," extended or built anew by the particular undertakers of the areas in which the sites were chosen. These stations, though owned and managed by such undertakers, would turn their whole output into a new grid or system of main transmission lines to be laid out by a new trading body—the Central Electricity Board—to the requirements of the technical Electricity Commissioners—and the managing undertakers would buy back current from the Board for their own requirements of direct distribution to consumers. The scheme was effective, and resulted, owing to the able and energetic efforts of the technicians and administrators who comprised the Board and the Commissioners, in the completion of the grid in about 1934. In the years immediately following, standardisation of pressure and frequency were achieved under the jurisdiction of the Commissioners; but the areas of distribution to consumers remained as they were. When war broke out in 1939 there had been two years of controversy over the proposals of the McGowan Committee of 1937 to carry reorganisation to a further stage by a "rationalisation" of undertakings so as to yield larger and better arranged areas of *distribution.*

After this compressed chronicle of events affecting the trading services between the two wars we come now to the current phase, inaugurated by measures passed by the Labour Government elected in 1945, and embodying its philosophy of public ownership. The Electricity Act of 1946 expropriated company and municipalities alike in order to integrate and re-organise the industry under a new structure of public ownership, based on a central authority and regional boards, specially appointed; the central authority taking over the control of generation and main transmission and the regional authorities the functions of distribution. The Gas Act of 1948 provided for the taking over of all gas undertakings by similar bodies, though in the different technical layout of the industry the regional authorities rather than the central will have the main operative functions in relation to plant. Whatever the reasons for this measure—and the Heyworth Committee of 1945 had drawn attention to the large number of small gas undertakings and advocated an integration of plant in better arranged areas of wider scope—it is worthy of note that there was not quite the same technical foundation for the measure as in the case of electricity. There is general agreement that nothing like the electricity grid is possible; and as gas can be stored, and electricity (for public supply purposes) cannot, there is not the same case for concentration of production so as to economise plant. Medium sized plants had in experience proved as economic as the larger.

As to road passenger transport undertakings, these were included in the scope of the Transport Act 1947, but the Act did not effect their wholesale transfer. Their destiny is to be the subject of area schemes to be formulated by the Transport Commission, which has control of all forms of transport within the scope of the measure. What is likely to happen is not yet clear; ad hoc authorities may be appointed for grouped undertakings; in some areas local authorities, or combinations of them, may be allowed to retain control. On the other hand, many of the aerodromes established by municipalities in the years before 1939 have been taken over by the Ministry of Civil Aviation under the Acts providing for civil aviation at the close of the war. The Labour Government left the supply of water to rest upon the provisions of an Act passed by the Coalition Government in 1944. This is not a nationalising measure; though it contains provisions designed to re-arrange areas and effect combinations, mergers, and the establishment of joint boards, etc., in conformity with a national plan for a better utilisation of resources and layout of distributive areas. Little has yet been achieved under this Act in the way of amalgamations.

Summarising now what has happened in the trading sphere, we see that of the four characteristic services, two (electricity and gas) are lost to new state agencies, one (local street transport) may be lost in whole or part, and only one (water) remains as a recognised municipal service, and even here a number of private undertakings are still in existence, and more Joint Boards may be formed. As a small set-off, municipalities were enabled to continue, on certain conditions, the "British Restaurants" for war-time communal feeding.

Added together, the local authorities' losses of function in the Social and Trading Services are heavy. The tale must be rounded off, moreover, by recording the loss of the ancillary service of valuation for rating, under provisions in the Local Government Act 1948 which transfer the responsibility to the Board of Inland Revenue and create new tribunals for appeal. It is not merely that local government is appreciably less in scope than it was in 1939. Lengthening the vista of retrospect, we may say, indeed, that the post-war years have brought local government the biggest set-back it has suffered since its beginnings in the early 19th century. After attaining a peak in 1939, it falls, or is about to fall in 1949, to a level of public provision less in ambit than that of the latter half of the last century, though a vast unclassified mass of regulative administration has accumulated which occupies its attention more than ever.

3. STRUCTURE

Without commenting on this situation at the moment, let us see what has happened to local government structure. The most striking fact is that there has been no change whatever in the units which comprise the structure, namely, the county borough, the county, the borough, the urban district, the rural district, and the rural parish (a situation which in itself goes far to explain the local authorities' sudden loss of functions after 1945). Indeed, the units remain of the same kind as were retained, or created, to form a general structure, when the Act of 1894 put the finishing touches to a system which had grown up piecemeal during the course of the nineteenth century and had previously included many types of ad hoc authority. The broad characteristic of this system is that a number of the larger towns, including the big cities, all of them styled county boroughs, are constituted authorities for the full range of local government services within their areas; and that, outside these large island areas, so to speak, functions are shared, in what are known as the county areas, between the county council and the borough or urban district council in urban areas, and between the county council and the rural district council in rural areas, with a further division in these latter between the rural district council and the parish meetings or councils. Between the boroughs and urban districts there is not much difference so far as the range of functions is concerned; the boroughs having, however, a constitution which, like that of the county boroughs, follows the model of the Municipal Corporations Act of 1835, and embraces a Mayor instead of a Chairman and a number of Aldermen elected by Councillors. The Local Government Act of 1933 introduced, however, a change in nomenclature by describing the boroughs, urban districts, and rural districts alike, as "county districts."

To say that the organs themselves have not been changed does not, however, mean that there have been no adjustments of areas, or mutations in the types of organ operating in them. In retrospect, however, even changes of this kind are not considerable. As matters stood in 1914 there had been remarkably few. There had been a certain spread of suburb around the towns. Quite a number of county boroughs and boroughs had secured extensions of boundary and sometimes absorbed adjoining urban or rural districts; and quite a number of urban districts had grown, and secured the prestige of borough status. To meet these changes, adjustments had been made by the central authorities, upon local initiative, under the cumbrous procedure then operative. But no great area problem as yet troubled the counties or the rural districts.

The new means of road transport which arose from the introduction of the petrol engine, and which affected local government in so many ways, as we shall later stress, set up an overflow of population from the towns, resulting in an enormous expansion of their suburbs, and even a suburbanisation of the countryside. Towns in the industrial provinces grew together, creating what we now call "conurbations." London expanded into the homogeneous urban agglomeration we now call Greater London. Everywhere, in the vicinity of great centres of population, rural parishes, in tracts of countryside hitherto remote, changed almost overnight into substantial urbanised areas. All these movements in the residential quartering of the people were accompanied, and, indeed, stimulated, by a growing substitution of electric for steam motive power in industry, allowing wider freedom in the choice of factory sites, and leading to a settlement and re-settlement of industry in out-town areas, and an accompanying development of houses, shops, and garages.

One of the first effects of these changing conditions was to set up a conflict between the counties and county boroughs over proposals by the former to bring within their boundaries the "over-spill" areas into which their populations had moved out, a course resisted by the county councils because it meant a severe loss of rateable value to them, not to speak of a loss of prestige. After many battles at Boundary Inquiries up and down the country, and in Parliamentary Committees adjudicating on County Borough Boundary Extension Bills, the county councils scored a victory by securing the sympathy of the Government and Parliament of the day, and an Act was passed in 1926 raising the qualifying level of population for future grants of county borough status from 50,000 to 75,000, and requiring the grant to be made in future by Act of Parliament only, and not by provisional order of the Ministry of Health. But the years following showed that the area pattern needed a more general re-adjustment to its related structure; and in the Local Government Act of 1929 opportunity was taken to deal with this aspect of local government, as well as the re-organisation of highway administration and the transfer of poor law functions to the counties and county boroughs to which reference has already been made, and the questions of local finance to be noticed later.

The Act of 1929 inaugurated a system of periodical review of districts by county councils, leaving however adjustments of county borough and borough boundaries to the older procedures and leaving county boundaries in the inviolate position they had enjoyed for so long. It secured a useful reduction in the number of local authorities, many of which even at that epoch were deemed too small. It also secured a useful tidying up of areas. But the growing international crisis and its impact upon local authority work, together with the eventual outbreak of war in 1939, precluded the further area reviews which the Act had contemplated.

Meanwhile, for some years past a number of writers on local

government had been drawing attention to the impact of the new conditions on local government structure; but neither the local nor the central authorities appeared to be greatly impressed by the necessity for more radical measures. During the war years, however, when the national mood prompted planning for post-war re-construction in so many directions, the subject of local government structure did receive considerable attention. All the associations of local authorities published reports on the subject. Most of these contemplated reforms much to the pattern of the type of local authority represented by the sponsoring body. Even the report of the Association of Municipal Corporations, though contemplating a different type of structure from the existing one, by a division of the country into "all-purpose" authorities and areas, was clearly inspired by a county borough outlook. On the other hand, the Labour Party and a Committee of the National Association of Local Government Officers published schemes which, although in strong contrast, contemplated a dual structure in which the organs at the higher level would embrace areas wider than anything typified by existing units.

The NALGO Committee had recommended in their report that whatever the shape of future local government structure should be there was need for a standing Boundary Commission through which periodical adjustments of the area pattern could be made in the light of a continuous national conspectus. This idea won general assent at the close of the war; and Parliament in the Local Government Boundary Commission Act of 1945 established such a standing Commission. In their first report the Commission presented a general picture of the area pattern as then existing, and drew attention in particular to the continuing existence of so many small authorities and the great disparities in the size and resources of local authorities even of the same type. In their second report they intimated that, although their Parliamentary mandate had confined their powers of adjustments of areas to the existing types of local authority (in accordance with a White Paper published by the Government in 1945 proposing that no attempt should be made in the immediate post-war period to create a new structure)

o   209

they themselves had arrived at the conclusion that more drastic alterations were required; and submitted their own recommendations. Into the nature of these it is impossible to go at any length here. Suffice it to say that the Commission did not propose any system of wide regional areas, but a re-organisation of county areas, entailing an enlargement in some cases and a breaking up in others, so as to create a two-tier system into which, with few exceptions, even the largest county boroughs would be thrown. With this development would also go the creation of more substantial secondary units in the new county areas.

The recommendations involved a redistribution of functions, and in this and other respects went beyond the Commissions' existing powers. Their report posed the question, therefore, whether they should be given additional authority to carry out a substantial reform, or left to make minor adjustments of a kind which they themselves thought inadequate and unsatisfactory. The Government gave its answer in the middle of 1949 by announcing its intention to seek the repeal of the Act of 1945 and wind up the Commission. A Bill to this effect is passing through Parliament as this chapter passes through the press. In introducing it the Government announced that they were themselves reviewing the structure and functions of local government but that there was no prospect of legislation in the present Parliament. In repealing the Act of 1945, the new Bill re-instates the review procedure introduced in 1929 and amended in some respects by the consolidating Local Government Act of 1933. But the reviews were suspended throughout the war-period 1939 to 1945, no change in fact resulted from the work of the Boundary Commission, and the Government have further announced that, pending new legislation, they will not in fact countenance interim changes under the review procedure, except to allow a minor boundary adjustment where a local authority's housing scheme passes beyond its own boundary. The problem can only grow more acute, and once more a solution is delayed.

Turning now to the distribution of functions as between the several types of authority, we find that practically the only change of significance between the two wars was the transfer of highway functions effected by the Act of 1929 and already referred to. The conclusion of the second war, however, set in train a whole series of quite drastic changes, all of them by way of transfer from boroughs or districts to the county councils in the county areas. In 1914, as previously, the most striking feature in the distribution of functions was the extent to which they were in the hands of the town authorities, whether large or small, and whether county boroughs ranging upwards from 50,000 to 1,000,000, or boroughs or urban districts ranging downwards from 50,000 to as little as 5,000 or less. Quite a number of comparatively small non-county boroughs maintained their separate police forces, and the ambulance and fire services were everywhere in the hands of boroughs and urban districts to the exclusion of the county. The boroughs and urbans, as well as the county boroughs, held the communal services in their full range. It was they which ran the trading services; and they too were the local authorities for housing, to the exclusion of the county. Most boroughs of 10,000 and urban districts of 20,000 (as at the 1901 census) had availed themselves of the provisions in Part III of the Education Act 1902 and become the authorities for elementary education (up to the age of 14) in their parts of the administrative county.

Such a situation was, of course, not surprising. It was in the towns that the need for most local government services had first arisen, or made itself visible, and had first been met during the preceding century before the county councils were established in 1888. Indeed, in 1914, the functions of the county councils were slender.

Inaugurating the post-war changes, the Education Act of 1944, in order to secure an integration of administration in county areas, and to meet difficulties which had arisen in school re-organisation in such areas, following upon the adoption of a new division of education into primary and secondary at the age of 11-plus, transferred the responsibilities of the Part III authorities (boroughs and urban districts) to the county councils; with provision for the exercise of delegated powers by "divisional executives," these, in a defined class of "excepted" larger districts, being the borough or district council itself, but elsewhere ad hoc bodies. Under the National Health Service of 1946 the county took over maternity and child welfare functions from such boroughs and districts as had previously exercised them in some parts of county areas. The county also became the authority for the provision of ambulances in displacement of all the boroughs and districts. The Police Act 1946 merged all non-county borough police forces into those of the county, subject to provisions under which even county and county borough forces could be combined under joint police authorities. The Fire Services Act 1947 fulfilled a Government pledge to restore this service to local authority control on the dissolution of the war-time National Fire Service, but restored it to the counties in place of the boroughs and districts which had been the authorities before the war. The Town and Country Planning Act 1947 for the first time established the county council as a planning authority, the boroughs and districts ceasing to be such.

If these re-shuffles of responsibility are taken together with the transfers to national responsibility already recorded, it is clear that the greatest impact has fallen upon the boroughs and districts as a class, and in particular upon those medium-sized town authorities (mainly between 20,000 and 50,000 population) which formerly had police, maternity and child welfare, education, fire brigade, ambulance, town and country planning, and valuation functions, and many of which, like the county boroughs, carried on trading undertakings. The counties, though they have lost their hospitals and institutions, have lost nothing in the trading sphere, since they rarely carried on trading services. On the other hand they have inherited a whole range of new responsibilities from the boroughs and districts. The range of functions of the county boroughs is still greater than that of the counties, including as it does environmental and other services still left in the hands of the boroughs and districts in the county areas; but the difference is no longer anything like what it was in 1914, or at any time during the expansion of local government functions between the two wars.

Though nearly all the re-shuffles mentioned have eventuated after the second war, there can be no doubt that they were impelled by conditions which arose between the two wars, notably by some of the factors we have mentioned, such as the change in methods of road transport, and the consequent demographic changes. It must be said, however, that finance also has had something to do with these re-shuffles. Apart from a policy of establishing a unified control, in order to eliminate the many difficult questions of co-ordination which arose under the division of responsibility between county and district, there was a growing recognition of the need to spread the charge of onerous services over wider areas than the boroughs and districts, as a general measure of relief to local authority finance in the smaller units.

4. FINANCE AND CENTRAL CONTROL

It is to the questions of finance and of central control that we now turn. In 1914 the standing aid to local government from central funds was given through the revenues from local taxation licences which Parliament had "assigned" in 1882, in the fond belief that this arrangement would effect a standing adjustment of central and local finance. The amount was ludicrously small compared with the figures which rule to-day, standing (in 1914) at about £7 million. Specific grants were successively introduced for specific services—police, education, and the incipient new social services. Here again, the aggregate was modest and the bulk of the cost of local authority services, apart from trading services, was met by rates. The total expenditure on revenue accounts of the local authorities in 1913/14 was £148 million; expenditure on trading and other remunerative properties accounted for £44½ million; and of the balance of £93½ million, £71 million was defrayed from rate revenues and about £22½ million was the total of Exchequer grants. Outstanding debt was £562 million. In the same year, incidentally, the ordinary expenditure provided for in the nation's Budget was £179 million—only a score of millions or so more than that of the local authorities, a comparison which, if one bears in mind the extent to which defence services entered into the Budget figure, forms a striking illustration of the extent to which public expenditure on public services in 1914 was local. In the year 1939-40 out of a total revenue expenditure of £578 million, £290 was raised from rates and £182 had accrued from Exchequer grants of all kinds. By 1943-44 the total of grants had exceeded the revenue from rates. The aggregate expenditure on revenue account was about £700 million (including some local charges for emergency services and trading outlay); and of the £516 million not accounted for by trading services, £227 million had come from the Exchequer and only £204 million from rates.

This transition reveals the financial crisis through which local government passed between the two wars. Bearing roughly half the cost of the developing social services, and, until 1934, practically the whole cost of poor law relief, including relief to the unemployed when unemployment stood at the gigantic proportions which ruled throughout the long period of acute economic depression between the wars, the local authorities saw their rates rising yearly after 1914 to ever higher levels. The levels attained phenomenal height in the areas most stricken by unemployment. The ratepayer-resident found his case hard enough; but industrialists and farmers claimed that as rates entered into cost of production the existing scale of expenditure on rate account was an intolerable burden on British industry which penalised it in competition and thus accentuated unemployment in a vicious circle. Thought began to move towards a policy which would spread rate charges, and at the same time secure what was thought to be administrative advantage by transfers of function from district to county; also towards measures of increased Exchequer relief which would, however, allow Parliament to control its extent more effectively than by a mere extension of the system of percentage grants. At the same time, the nation began to realise how inequitable it was to leave the ratepayers in the badly stricken areas to bear so large a share of a national burden out of local resources. And at length came a realisation that the problem of local government finance was not only one of aggregate burden, but one of striking inequality of resources through disparities in rateable value which made some local authorities fortuitously rich and others fortuitously poor.

Meeting the arguments of the industrialists and farmers, the Act of 1929 granted a three-quarter rebate on rating valuations to defined classes of industrial and freight transport hereditaments, in addition to the relief which had been granted by the Rating and Valuation Act of 1925 through the de-rating of motive plant. Agricultural land and buildings (already enjoying a three-quarter rebate) it exempted altogether. The grants through assigned revenues were (with a few exceptions) abolished, together with some but not all of the more recent percentage grants. To meet the loss of revenues arising from these several provisions, the Act introduced a General Exchequer Contribution, that is to say a general block grant, the future level of which would periodically be settled by Parliament after being initially fixed to provide the local authorities with £50 million or so of new money after their de-rating losses had been recouped. The Act also contained provisions of a novel kind for the distribution of the grant to the local authorities. It applied for this purpose an elaborate formula which took into account the local incidence of unemployment, the proportion of children under school age, and the burden of maintaining roads in sparsely populated areas; thus recognising, in a measure, the problem of unequal resources and special burdens.

After the second war, however, the problem of finance had again to be dealt with by a major measure. Most of the authorities' war-time expenditure on civil defence had been met from central funds, and owing to war-time restrictions on normal work most of the authorities had accumulated substantial balances by the end of the war. But the accumulation of maintenance work, the increase in prices, and the demand for enhanced standards of provisions in so many services, called for a re-consideration of the whole position when the block grant became due for review under the legislation of 1929, after being postponed for several years through war-time conditions. The National Assistance Act of 1948, achieving the final break-up of the poor law, itself lifted millions of poor law costs from the shoulders of the local authorities; but the Local Government Act of 1948 also made additions to the Block Grant and set it upon a new footing, designed to meet the problem of inequality in local authority resources, by providing that, in its future distribution, local authorities whose rateable value fell below the average for the country should receive a compensating heavier apportionment, the intention being that by this means the old contrasts between rich and poor local authorities should largely disappear.

If there is any virtue in the old principle "that he who pays the piper may call the tune" it is not to be wondered at that the increasing central assistance has been accompanied by increasing central control. In the services aided by percentage grants the central authority has, of course, always required that its approval should be sought to the estimated expenditure; and the general requirements of central approval to capital expenditure, through loan sanction, is a requirement which has persisted throughout the period under review as one of the fundamental controls exercised over local government in general. The process has, however, not stopped here. The services aided by specific grants are mainly those in which, from a political angle, the local authority is acting as an agent for the State in the maintenance of services which are in fact national. In the period under review national sentiment has favoured the establishment of something like uniform standards in each area. As a consequence, the central authorities have greatly developed the controls which they exercise over these services through the medium of statutory rules and regulations made under the authority of the Acts of Parliament. It is only right to say, however, that the introduction of the Block Grant in 1929 did entail a substantial modification of previous philosophy as to the nexus which should rule between control and aid. The Block Grant may have regard to particular services but it is a general grant-in-aid not earmarked to such services, and entails no new specific control over them. When first introduced in 1929 the Block Grant was opposed in Parliament on the ground that it was designed to set limits to the scope of the social services. It is clear, however, that it had administrative advantages in setting the local authorities free of further detailed controls in the general expansion of central aid; and it is noteworthy that the Labour Government continued the device on a revised footing in its measure of 1948.

Finally, we may note that central control has expanded even apart from increased central financial aid. What was happening between the two wars was that a number of services, notably in the trading sphere, in ways we have shown, were being fitted into a framework of national policy designed to improve the layout on which they had grown up as local enterprises. There was at that stage no unification of ownership; but before eventually passing over, under the nationalisation measures which brought such a unification, many of the services had in fact become subject to many forms of national control exercised through the Ministries.

5. THE UNDERLYING CAUSES OF CHANGE

Our review has shown that the really extensive changes over the whole period have occurred in the last few years following the close of the second war. Enough has been said already, however, to indicate that in the main the causes which shaped the changes arose at a much earlier period. They first made themselves manifest in the beginning of the period we have under review and operated with increasing potency in the period between the two wars. The changes of 1945-9 really represent a belated response to needs and difficulties accumulating throughout the inter-war period ; and these needs and difficulties sprang for the most part from changes in the distribution of population and changes in technological conditions, the former being in many cases attributable to the latter.

Beyond all doubt the most important factor was the development of the petrol engine and its application to road transport, with the demographic consequences already noted. Without attempting to be exhaustive, let us recapitulate some of the manifold ways in which this change alone affected local government. The changes in highways administration of 1929 and 1936 accrued because the roads of Great Britain, which the railway age has relegated to but a minor rôle in the system of communications, assumed a new importance; one which called for their thorough re-habilitation and the re-adjustment of administrative arrangements which had left the planning of them largely unprovided for, and the responsibility for their maintenance dispersed among a multitude of local authorities of which many were too small to sustain the costly work now needed. The outspread of population affected the standards and administrative arrangements for the provision of schools and other social services, and called for a new concept of environmental planning. Local road passenger transport was transmogrified from trams to 'buses. Electricity, gas, and water services were called upon to serve outlying areas and link town with town. The movements of population created on the one hand large conurbations, though the linking of communities hitherto separate and the filling in of the intervening spaces with building development, while on the other hand, and at the same time, they represented a scattering of population and an urbanisation of rural areas. Many of the smaller communities, urban and rural, no longer remained isolated. The very difference between urban and rural was blurred. All these events called for re-adjustment of areas, and in the opinion of many left the structure itself outmoded. Added to the development in transport, with all the consequences that it brought in its train, were other technical developments such as those in electricity supply, increasing the area in which generation could take place, and the effects of the petrol engine upon the transport service itself, no longer leaving the typical undertaking as an octopoid of tram-lines radiating from a town centre.

On top of all this came the financial crisis, occasioned by the deficiencies of local finance in the expansion of services, and the mass unemployment it had been called upon to sustain.

What should be noted in particular, and what could be amply demonstrated by a more detailed survey, is this: that all of these pressures, and not merely one or other of them, were pressures in the direction of larger areas for local government purposes. In the last analysis the same causes which forced a re-shuffle of responsibilities from boroughs and districts to counties, are those which did much to force the transfer from local government of the hospitals, electricity undertakings, and gas works. All these factors, again, were factors which, in the conditions indicated, inevitably brought about increased and expanded central control over the local authorities. The new conditions demanded integration: integration of services, both as to standards and lay-out; integration of areas left artificially divided; integration of services which had grown up piecemeal. And the agency of integration had inevitably to be central control, even at the stages before some of the services passed out of local hands altogether.

We begin to see something of the dilemma in which the Labour Government was placed at the close of the war. Granted its principle of public ownership, could it have kept such services as hospitals, electricity, and gas within the sphere of local government? Despite all critics the answer must be "No." The general structure of local government had not been kept on a footing which could accommodate the services in their new shape and with their new requirements for larger areas, or which could assimilate satisfactorily the units hitherto in private ownership. Hence the spectacle of a Party which, in its missionary days, had preached an expanded municipalism as one of its major objectives, becoming an instrument for the greatest curtailment of local government functions which has taken place for 150 years.

Could the structure of local government have been adapted so as to retain such services? Those who for many years previously had preached regionalism, or some alternative providing wider areas, would claim to-day that it could, if their principles had been applied. They believe the adoption of their principles to be no less urgent now than in the past if we are to prevent similar happenings in future. Some of them cherish a hope that, with an enlarged structure, local government may regain the services lost. This seems a remote possibility, because the services will have taken their own new administrative impress from the new agencies which now control them, and their lay-out will have been shaped to their own requirements. Whether, with their new characteristics, they could subsequently be fitted into even a reformed local government structure is, to say the least of it, very doubtful indeed.

No doubt the services concerned will eventually gain from the improved lay-out they may now expect. Even from an administrative point of view, however, the gain will be accompanied by some loss. The municipal committee table did a lot for efficiency in providing a focal point at which control, management and consumer representation found ready contact, and at which each could realise the others' needs and problems. The consumer had an access and a leverage which the new forms of administration do not visibly, and cannot readily be made to, provide. The new services must now assemble their own specialised staffs, but it is doubtful whether "tool" and "agency" departments will be provided as economically in cost and man-power as when the Town Clerk, the Treasurer, the Architect, the Engineer, and the other specialised staffs of a substantial local authority ministered to a variety of trading and other services. We must also remember that it is often an important element in service to the consumer to supply one need in co-ordination with another. There may well be gain in co-ordination within each particular service and a loss of that general area co-ordination which was the inseparable virtue of unified municipal control.

Nor are the successive and extensive transfers from borough and district to county responsibility an ideal solution of the problems of local government they were designed to meet. In the extreme disparities that still exist in the size, not only of the boroughs and districts but of the counties themselves, and in the prevalent maladjustment of status and boundaries to area characteristics, automatic transfer according to status is bound to have entailed almost as many anomalies and administrative misfits as were involved in the original allocation on these lines. If many existing districts and boroughs were too small for the exercise of the functions now transferred, not all of them were, or may remain so after even a moderate reform of areas. Nor can the relevant administrative or representative considerations be satisfactorily met by a process which transfers functions to counties which are as widely uneven in size as

18,000 population at the one extreme, and 2,000,000 at the other, and whose boundaries have received less attention in the past than those of any other type of authority.

6. TODAY AND TOMORROW

The cardinal feature in our review is the dwindled scope and importance of local self-government; carrying with it a corresponding loss of the educative influence local government has had in the past, and which has done so much for our social progress and stability, and taken the raw edge off the sharper conflicts of class and creed by bringing men of widely different mind and station in life into practical co-operative work for their local communities. The situation is due to a failure to keep on foot a suitable general structure, when conditions arose which called for reform in many directions and in particular for the introduction of a wider kind of unit and area, and when the choice or rejection of local government agencies for the provision or conduct of public services came more and more to be decided on purely administrative grounds. The responsibility is very far from being that of one political party and some of it is attributable to the local authorities themselves, who were blind to the situation for too long.

The philosophy we referred to in our introduction persists, and is responsible for some of the disquiet now felt, but it carries less weight than it did. We hear from high quarters that the question of local government functions is not one of providing a structure and then allocating suitable functions, but of considering the functions and then assigning them to the most suitable administrative agencies. "Whate'er is best administered is best." This attitude might be justified if we had reached a stage when the educative force, and the salutary disciplines, of local self-government could be disregarded. But can we be so sure that the present generation stands so much less in need of *this* kind of tutelage than its predecessors did?

Finally, we must regret the narrowing prospect for the exercise of the local initiative which built up local government, and did so much for the nation throughout the nineteenth and early twentieth centuries. The Labour Party in power has shown no sign of introducing the measure which the Labour Party in opposition introduced into successive Parliaments, namely, the Local Authorities Enabling Bill, which would have allowed local authorities to undertake any enterprise not specifically reserved for central government or private agencies, in abrogation of the principle of allowing local authorities to exercise only those powers and functions which Parliament expressly confers. So large a reversal of past policy is not likely to win acceptance. In any event all the conditions of the time are against it. The present levels of national economy will hardly permit of unrestricted licence to provide local amenities which may not be absolutely essential from a national standpoint. The local authorities have now a much less capacious financial reservoir. In the change of money values, their rating resources, even taking into account the relief afforded by central financial help, no longer afford a large freedom for local initiative. The prospect, then, for any return of the freedom and experiment which marked local government until so recently does not seem very bright. Can we be sure that such a situation may safely continue?

We have certainly a wider choice of available agencies of public administration to-day than in the past, when choice was a matter of a simple dichotomy between departments like the Post Office on the one hand and the local authorities on the other. The machinery for centralised administration is undoubtedly more efficient, varied, and adaptable in this century than in the last. From its very nature, however, it may be responsive to public needs only along well-beaten tracks; whereas it would be surprising if a high proportion of social changes did not arise unforeseen and first make themselves manifest and felt in the lives of local communities, for this was our experience throughout the last century. Society is never static. The need for local improvisation may arise once more. So much more important is it, therefore, on all these considerations, that the spirit of local initiative and responsibility, the sense of local community, and the process of mutual education that springs from the co-operation of groups classes and individuals in the provision of communal needs, should not be allowed to perish because they lack suitable organs, adapted to the needs of the time, endowed with adequate power, and possessing a wide freedom for real initiative.

For Product Safety Concerns and Information please contact our EU
representative GPSR@taylorandfrancis.com
Taylor & Francis Verlag GmbH, Kaufingerstraße 24, 80331 München, Germany

www.ingramcontent.com/pod-product-compliance
Lightning Source LLC
Chambersburg PA
CBHW070240290326
41929CB00046B/2269

9 781032 889290